Giving U.P.

Giving U.P.: A New Understanding & Perspective of The Bible
Copyright© 2025 by Lionel P. Wesley
All rights reserved. This book or any portion thereof may not be reproduced or used in any manner whatsoever without the express written permission of the publisher except for the use of brief quotations in a book review.

Limits of Liability and Disclaimer of Warranty
The author and publisher shall not be liable for your misuse of this material. This book is strictly for informational purposes. The purpose of this book is to educate. The author and publisher do not guarantee anyone following these techniques, suggestions, tips, ideas, or strategies will become successful. The author and publisher shall have neither liability nor responsibility to anyone with respect to any loss or damage caused, or alleged to be caused, directly or indirectly by the information contained in this book. Views expressed in this publication do not necessarily reflect the views of the publisher.

Printed in the United States of America
Keen Vision Publishing, LLC
www.publishwithkvp.com
ISBN: 979-8-9927392-5-1

A NEW UNDERSTANDING & PERSPECTIVE OF THE BIBLE

LIONEL P. WESLEY

CONVERSATIONS INSIDE
TO BE EXPERIENCED IN NO PARTICULAR ORDER

Introduction	7
Conversation 1: The Timeline of Creation	11
Conversation 2: God's Creation of Humans	17
Conversation 3: Eve and Adam's Fall	23
Conversation 4: The Blessing of Abraham	39
Conversation 5: The Wilderness	47
Conversation 6: God's Love and The Point of Soul Development	55
Conversation 7: On Earth As It is In Heaven	85
Conversation 8: Mankind's Continued Documentation	91
Conversation 9: John the Baptist	107
Conversation 10: Remain in Your Baptism	115
Conversation 11: Purpose	121
About the Author	124

INTRODUCTION

To professional academics, scholars, and theologians, this work may seem shallow. To some creationists and Christians, it may sound non-biblical or even blasphemous. To atheists and Gnostics, it might mean nothing at all—perhaps mildly entertaining. But to everyone in between, and to those standing on the fence with their faith, this may be something worth seriously thinking about.

There is a widespread lack of understanding when it comes to the scriptures. Sometimes, it stems from a lack of revelation—which, in truth, is God's timing, not a personal failure. Other times, it's due to the loss of meaning that naturally happens when sacred texts are translated across languages and cultures. Again, this is not something to be ashamed of—it's part of the process of seeking and learning.

Too often, people only view the Bible through the lens of what they hear on Sunday from a church or temple leader.

Others don't consider the Bible at all. Some never make the time to dig deeper, while others believe there's nothing more to learn beyond what their pastor teaches. Whatever the reason, the result is the same—many miss the profound, life-giving lessons the Bible offers.

This is not an indictment of church leaders. I recognize that priests, preachers, and teachers are often limited in time and must tailor their messages to the needs of their congregation or the theme of the service. But there is more. And my hope is that this work—this discussion—will lead you to explore the Word of God from a broader and deeper perspective.

I don't write this to turn anyone away from faith in our Savior and Redeemer. On the contrary, I write to draw those who are confused about the ways of our Creator—or who feel torn between scientific reasoning and biblical history—closer to God. I believe science and faith can coexist, and in many cases, they already do. While not everything can or should be explained by human understanding, God reveals truths to us at the appointed time.

This work is not intended to spark arguments or stir up debates over trivialities that do nothing to glorify God. Instead, it's meant to provoke thoughtful reflection, to challenge assumptions, and to help draw people into a deeper love for the Creator.

Throughout this manuscript, I will refer to our Lord and Savior as Jesus or Christ. I recognize that names such as Jeshua, Jehoshua, Joshua, Yehoshu'ah (Yehoshuah), Yeshu'ah (Yeshua), Iesus, Iēsous, and Isho are all historically and linguistically valid. I'm reminded of a scene from the movie, *Coming to America*, where the men in the barbershop debated over what to call the boxer Muhammad Ali. One barber finally said, *"His momma called him Clay. I'm gonna call him Clay."* I know His mother, Mary (Myriam or Maryam), most likely called Him Yehoshuah or Yeshua—the Aramaic and Hebrew forms of His name. But for the sake of clarity and consistency in this work, I will refer to Him as Jesus.

This journey is an invitation. If you approach this with an open heart and mind, you're likely to discover new layers of meaning—some challenging, some affirming, all designed to point you back to the heart of God. Let this be more than just reading. Let it be a reflection. A conversation. A path toward deeper faith. Together, let's begin the process of *Giving U.P.*—letting go of long-held myths and assumptions, and gaining a new Understanding and Perspective of the Bible. The goal isn't to abandon truth, but to pursue it more boldly, more honestly, and more fully than ever before.

GIVING U.P.
Thoughts

Conversation One
THE TIMELINE OF CREATION
Was seven days REALLY enough to get the job done?

You may wonder, *"Who cares how long it took God to create the world? People need to know about Jesus!"* And while I wouldn't argue with that sentiment, the reality is that MANY care about the timeline of Creation. For MANY, the math found in Genesis does not add up, and it is hard to keep reading towards the New Testament to find out about Jesus. Sadly, MANY disregard the Bible because of the Creation timeline. Upon hearing the argument that God created the Earth around 5,000 years ago, in six 24-hour days, they decide not to believe anything else in the Bible, throwing the baby out with the bath water. Therefore, we begin our journey of Giving U.P. where it all began: CREATION. Whether you are sure of your stance about the timeline of Creation or are among the many who have questions, let this conversation challenge you to gain a newer and deeper perspective about God, your Creator.

When viewing things like Creation, humanity, and mankind's purpose, it is vital to remember that everything must start and end with God. As a believer and follower of Christ, or anyone looking for answers about their purpose, the focus should always revolve around the Lord. The focus should never be centered on man, woman, or any other created being. It is all about the Creator, His kingdom of eternity, and most importantly, His love for us. God's love has a purpose and intent for each of us. Keep this at the forefront of your mind as you read.

It is probable that the idea of the world being created in more than seven days isn't as far-fetched or blasphemous as it seems. Although the seven-day creation period is possible with our God, it may extend across a different length of time. The period of Creation most likely exceeded the 144 hours (6 days) that some Biblical theologians recognize. Scientific and theological perspectives support this argument, and we will discuss both views in this conversation about Creation's timeline.

According to most theologians' understanding of the Bible, the sixth day of Creation was quite busy. After creating Adam, God placed him in the garden. Then, God brought the animals to Adam to name (Genesis 2:19). After recognizing that it was not good for man to be alone, God put Adam to sleep and fashioned Eve. Think about that short length of time. Think about the number of animals Adam had to name. Think about the time or situations that took place to cause God to recognize man needed a companion. So, was Eve truly created on the 6th day? According to scripture,

Adam had already been living and walking with God for a little while before Eve entered the garden. It could've been a 24-hour day, and it could've been over a few days or weeks. Why is this relevant when discussing the true timeline of Creation? It matters because if these events took place over a few days or weeks, we must rethink our idea of the 24-hour, 7-day point of view.

WORDS MATTER

An alternate *seven days* theory could be seven periods or seven ages. This change in the wording and meaning of the term *day* used in Genesis aligns with scientific data and historical findings on the approximate age of the Earth. Archeological findings, prehistoric events, and data discovered by carbon dating would agree with the truth that God created the heavens and the Earth over a greater span of time than seven days.

Moses wrote in his Psalm 90 prayer, *"A thousand years in Your sight are like yesterday when it passes by or as a watch in the night."* Peter wrote in 2 Peter 3:8, *"With the Lord, one day is like a thousand years and a thousand years like one day."* So, when the Lord was describing or, better put, revealing the Creation to Moses, He may have used a day to describe the period, even though it could've been a thousand or even a million years as we recognize it today. So, even from a theological standpoint, the *day* referred to in Genesis is not a day that we would refer to as a 24-hour day.

I am not advocating for the Bible to be rewritten. I don't believe that the Bible should be changed to fit mankind's comfort or understanding. Our comfort and understanding must always conform to our Creator's. If the word given to Moses translates to a day, then that is what God wanted Moses to use. However, it is possible that God's day of Creation could correspond to thousands or millions of years in human time, as Moses and Peter wrote in their perspective of God's time.

LIGHT CHANGES EVERYTHING

From a theological perspective, what was the light source for the first three days? The sun and moon were not created until the fourth day. We know from Genesis 1:2 that the Earth was formless and void, so there was no rotation of the Earth and no movement of the greater and lesser lights to indicate our evenings and mornings as we now know it. Also, a person on Earth would not have had the reference of the sun or moon the first three days to declare that the day took place in 24 hours. Therefore, the days, evenings, and mornings, as we now know it, are not the same days, evenings, and mornings Moses is writing about. What does this all mean? This means we can look at the language and words used in Genesis from an unfamiliar perspective rather than the literal, as many choose to do.

The Earth's early light source has been the center of theologians' and scholars' creation timeline debates for millennia. Tertullian (155-220 AD), an early apologist and theologian, believed that the light was a physical manifestation of Christ's glory. Ephrem (306-373 AD), an apologist, hymnographer, and theologian, believed the light was a huge bright mist. Basil (329-379 AD), the Bishop of Caesarea in Cappadocia, believed that the light was the essence of the sun, with its physical substance coming on Day 4. Augustine of Hippo (354-430 AD) believed that angels in their heavenly bodies/glory were the first light shining over the Earth.[1]

Like Tertullian, I believe that the original light was Christ. The Bible tells us that Christ was present at Creation and that all Creation starts with Him (John 1:3, 10; Colossians 1:16). Also, Revelation tells us that Christ will eventually take the place of the sun as the light of the Earth, *"there will be no need for lamps or the light of the sun."* (Revelation 22:5) It is fitting that the first light the world had at Creation would be the last light that will shine upon its face.

Most scientists agree that the sun must have been created before the Earth. Dr. Hugh Ross, an astrophysicist, does not disagree, but he provides an explanation for the timing of the greater light and lesser light's visibility from the Earth. In his book, The Genesis Question, Dr. Ross explains that the story of Creation was written from the point of reference of a person viewing the Creation from Earth. The sun and moon were not mentioned until Day 4 because the Earth's atmosphere was covered in such a dark, cloudy mist that a person could not see the light from the sun or moon until the dark mist dissipated from the atmosphere. There are similarities in the theological perspective of Basil, the Bishop of Caesarea, and the scientific perspective of Dr. Ross.

As we close this conversation, consider this question:

---

1 [https://answersingenesis.org/days-of-creation/days-without-sun-what-was-source-light/]

Why the rush? The Bible states, in Genesis, that as God spoke, the Spirit, who was waiting and hovering, gave life to the Lord's words. Is it possible that giving life to God's words may have taken more time than we once originally perceived? Is it possible that God took His time developing the universe, animals, and mankind? The Bible supports this notion. God takes time in preparing our blessings for us, like in the case of Israel entering the Promised Land, Joseph gaining power in Egypt, Abraham and Sarah having a baby, and Jesus being born after the "Silent Years" (400 years of "silence" between the Old Testament and New Testament events). Just because our God can complete the events of Creation within a seven-day period does not mean that He had to do it in that time. Like many of the amazing works of God, Creation most likely took time.

Whether your eyes have been opened or you remain unsure, allow your questions to take you on a quest that brings you closer to God and develops more awe of His wonder-working power. And never forget that the greatest revelation you could find in all 66 books is Christ's purpose and love for you.

Conversation Two

GOD'S CREATION OF HUMANS

Did God create more than the two?

Have you ever wondered if Adam and Eve were truly the only humans God formed at the dawn of creation, or could the Lord's work have extended far beyond that first pair? Many people assume that Adam and Eve were the sole origin of the entire human race. Yet the details within Scripture can raise challenging questions about whether they were truly the only people God created. As this conversation unfolds, allow your mind to remain open to fresh perspectives and possibilities. Remember that each inquiry about our beginnings points back to God's ultimate plan, love, and sovereignty.

CAIN'S FEAR: "WHOEVER FINDS ME WILL KILL ME"

Consider the idea that Adam and Eve were not the only humans God created. Along with that possibility, there is also the notion that Cain, Abel, and Seth did not need to marry their own sisters, nor did the entire earth have to be populated by one family alone.

Genesis 4 describes the story of Cain and Abel. After Cain killed Abel, and God cursed the ground that Cain would walk on, Cain tells the Lord, "*It will come about that whoever* (some manuscripts use the words 'anyone who') *finds me will kill me*" (verses 11–14). Notice how *whoever* or *anyone who* are words typically used to refer to strangers or unknown persons, not immediate family or even distant relatives.

Cain is identified as Adam and Eve's first documented child, likely the oldest. As the firstborn, he would know all his siblings and their children. At this time, the ground had not been cursed for Cain or for the first humans, so there was no need for them to roam. They could all remain in the same location. The fact that Cain and Abel were close enough to interact, and that Eve desired another child after Abel's death, suggests the *first family* were all in proximity to one another. Thus, Cain would have known all his siblings and their children at the time of God's curse.

Furthermore, if every inhabitant of the earth at that time was a direct descendant of Adam and Eve, then Cain, as the oldest, would have been the first to father a child with one of his sisters—or Abel would have done so if Cain had not. In that scenario, the *whoever* or *anyone* Cain spoke of would have been his own nieces and nephews. He would have known them, since they all lived near each other. Additionally, the curse applied only to Cain, not to the rest of his family, so the others would have had no reason to wander or interact with him as he and his wife traveled (verse 17). Given these points, it is a reasonable argument that God could have created other men and women aside from Adam and Eve, and these people represent the *whoever* and *anyone* in verses 11–14.

But Cain's dilemma is not the only question tied to the earliest generations. Another issue centers on Eve's role as *mother of all the living,* and how it might fit with the possibility of additional humans.

ADDRESSING EVE AS "MOTHER OF ALL THE LIVING"

If all humanity is believed to come solely from Adam and Eve, it then follows that Adam and Eve must have had daughters for Cain, Abel, and Seth to marry and populate the earth. One might assume that Adam had relations only with Eve, never with his own daughters. However, Scripture does not record the birth of a girl or any daughters to Adam and Eve. In the same vein, Scripture need not necessarily document God creating additional people elsewhere. An opposing viewpoint may reference Genesis 3:20:

> *Now the man called his wife's name Eve, because she was the mother of all the living.*

The Hebrew words for "Eve" (Chavah, to cover, protect, or hide) and "mother of all the living" (em kol chi) carry distinct meanings. Chaim Bentorah elaborates on Eve's name:

> *The word chavah as the mother of all life expresses not only the ability to give birth to life but also to nourish and enhance all facets of this physical life.*[2]

---

2 [https://www.chaimbentorah.com/2021/11/Hebrew-word-study-eve-chavah-%d7%97%d7%95%d7%94/]

When Adam named Eve, he was not necessarily claiming that she herself was the direct mother of all living. Rather, he was acknowledging that through woman (females in general), life would be generated, protected, and nurtured. He was not stating that all life would eventually stem from Eve alone. Clearly, she was not the mother of Adam, nor of animals, fish, or plants, so the words need not be taken in a strictly literal sense.

If Eve's title does not automatically mean that every human descends solely from her, the issue of maintaining the family line without close-kin relationships comes into focus next.

THE INCEST QUESTION

This naturally leads to the question of how the earliest families multiplied and spread out if Adam and Eve did not have daughters—or if marrying within the same bloodline was never God's intention. Leviticus 18:7–18 (Mosaic Law) explicitly forbids incest, labeling it detestable. Thousands of years before Moses, Abraham's marriage to his stepsister Sarah (Sarai) demonstrates that incest was allowed at some level, but a closer look at Scripture suggests it may never have been fully acceptable.

Genesis 19:30–38 recounts Lot's daughters, who felt compelled to intoxicate their father so they could conceive children with him in a cave, aiming to preserve the family line (Genesis 19:32). While their goal was understandable, the question arises: if incest was wholly acceptable at that time, why get their father drunk? A man typically welcomes an opportunity to continue his lineage. If there had been no moral conflict, their plan would not have required deception. Similarly, Cain's offering in Genesis (no written law existed then) was deemed unacceptable not because of a technical rule, but because his heart and attitude were wrong. It implies humanity possessed an inner understanding of right and wrong even before the Law.

If incest was never truly God's intention, it is plausible that He created additional people so that Adam and Eve's children—and later Noah's descendants—would not be forced to look within their own families for spouses. This approach addresses potential moral and logistical concerns surrounding close-kin marriage.

Yet the early accounts in Genesis do not stop with Adam, Eve, and Cain. The story moves forward dramatically after the Flood, revealing another phase in which God might have continued creating humans.

POST-FLOOD PARALLELS AND THE SPREAD OF HUMANITY

The same argument that God might have created other humans during Adam and Eve's era can also apply after the Flood. Although God effectively *started over* with Noah's family, the same divine purpose seen with Adam and Eve's family from the beginning remained intact: to deliver the message of God's love and intention for humanity, including the vital link of the Savior to the earliest humans. Noah's family was responsible for preserving and passing on the story of humankind's beginnings and the lineage of the Lord—not merely for repopulating the earth. Scripture from both Old and New Testaments reveals the continuous story of man, culminating in the Son of Man, Jesus.

Just as other individuals may have existed during the time of Adam, Eve, and Cain, other humans may have been created after the flood as well. Those newly created people would possess an inherent awareness of a higher power and likely have natural skills to survive, work the land, and fulfill certain responsibilities. However, it was through Noah's family—eyewitnesses to God's power and deeply devoted to the Lord—that the narrative of divine love and salvation would be carried forward.

This post-Flood backdrop sets the stage for one of the Bible's most enigmatic events: the Tower of Babel, where humanity's ambition confronted God's command to fill the earth.

TRIBALISM AND THE TOWER OF BABEL

When God created man and woman, intelligence was inherently placed in them. Genesis 2:19–20 and 23 highlight Adam's ability to name the animals and his wife. Naming in Old Testament culture often entailed defining a being's nature or future. Adam's task of cultivating the garden likewise demanded a level of understanding and capability not associated with immaturity or ignorance, indicating that Adam and Eve possessed a foundational intelligence at creation. After Adam and Eve ate from the tree of the knowledge of good and evil and their eyes were opened, God could have granted that same measure of insight to other humans He created. It is feasible that the Lord also established villages or tribes of people in one region to encourage communal living, often referred to as tribalism.

This idea of ongoing creation might explain why the story of the Tower of Babel (Genesis 11) appears amid the account of Noah's descendants. The swift repopulation of the earth could have involved more than just Noah's lineage.

Some might question the placement of the Tower of Babel narrative in the middle of the genealogy of Shem (Noah's son), suggesting there was more happening than just Noah's family story. Historians vary in opinion as to how long after the Flood this took place—some say around 100 years, others around 700 years. This pause in Noah's family line may indicate that other intelligent populations existed apart from Noah's direct descendants.

Historical evidence suggests that great strides in agriculture and urban development were emerging in diverse parts of the world—such as the Americas, northern Europe, and east Asia—relatively soon after the flood. These advancements could be attributed to the God-given intelligence humans have possessed since the time of Adam and Eve.

Yet records also reveal that many of these emerging populations did not acknowledge or glorify God. Perhaps Noah's descendants had not yet shared their testimony, or perhaps it had become diluted by legends of other gods. Whatever the reasons, it is clear that large groups of people existed who did not center their lives around the Lord.

The Babel event underscores God's desire for humanity to spread across the globe, leading us to examine precisely why He intended people to fill the earth and share His story.

THE PURPOSE OF FILLING THE EARTH

Critics of this viewpoint often cite verses like Genesis 9:19 and Genesis 10:32, which state that from Noah's sons *"the whole earth was populated."* They may also point to Acts 17:26—*"and He made from one every nation of mankind to live on all the face of the earth..."* However, it is possible that Noah's sons and their descendants simply spread out and became founding leaders of diverse nations, as Acts 17:27 affirms they had a purpose in testifying of God to their families and tribes. These descendants most likely shared their personal accounts of God's power and order with others that the Lord created. God could have instilled in these newer populations the inclination to follow or collaborate with Noah's lineage, so that all nations would seek Him. They would seek the one true God, the Creator of all, the God of the flood, under the spiritual guidance of Noah's family, who had experienced God's might firsthand.

Looking more closely at the Tower of Babel narrative, the people cooperated peacefully and wanted to remain unified, but their goals directly contradicted God's commands. They strove to make their own name and nation the center of honor rather than the Lord's—an idolatry rooted in pride. They also refused to disperse, attempting instead to settle together and construct a tower at a place later known as Babel (from the Hebrew *balal*, meaning to mingle, mix, or confuse). Though God values human unity, He never intended for people to cease exploring creation. He commanded Noah's descendants to *"fill the earth"* (Genesis 9:1). The world needed their testimony because other groups that God formed did not possess firsthand knowledge of the Lord's love and discipline. Without Noah's descendants' account, the world would lack accurate knowledge to give God the honor He expects.

This command to fill the earth highlights the deeper principle of free will and faith—choices that determine humanity's willingness to follow God or seek alternatives.

THE ROLE OF FAITH AND CHOICE

Why operate in this manner? Why select certain individuals to convey the divine story? While it may be challenging to comprehend, the reasoning is straightforward: people need alternatives to recognize the goodness they possess, the goodness they could gain, and the goodness they lost. Humanity must have the capacity to choose between God and an alternative. Such choice involves faith, and faith is essential to please the Lord (Hebrews 11:6). This plan for humanity's learning rests on that principle.

Like those living in Adam and Eve's era, any populations God created after the flood would have sensed an inner call toward a higher being, but lacked a concrete image of the one true God. Noah's family alone could supply that living testimony—an eyewitness account of God's saving grace through the Flood. People might intuit a divine presence, but needed something solid to anchor their faith: the Flood story relayed through Noah's descendants. Even as people scattered and took on varied identities, Scripture affirms that all nations share a common lineage under one Creator—a truth highlighted in Acts 17:26.

ACTS 17:26 AND OUR COMMON SOURCE

The verses in Genesis 9 and 10 have been addressed, but Acts 17:26 also raises questions. Various manuscripts translate it as *from one, from one man, from one blood,* or *from one family.* Many theologians believe this refers to Adam as humanity's root.

In Acts 17, Paul indirectly confronted the cultural snobbery of the era. Jews classified everyone as either Jew or Gentile, Romans as citizens or non-citizens, and Greeks as Greeks or barbarians—essentially dividing the world into *us* and *them.* Paul explained that all races share a single Creator, specifically from the lineage of Adam. His intent was to show that the one true, living God formed every person from the same flesh and blood as the first intellectual man, Adam. This concept echoes throughout Scripture and is underscored by Malachi 2:10 (NASB 1995):

Do we not all have one father? Has not one God created us?

Acts 17:26 can be understood in another way: just as God used one rib from Adam to form Eve, He could have used a single drop of Adam's blood or a single hair follicle to form additional people. Modern medical science requires only a small amount of genetic material to produce new life within a woman's womb, and God certainly does not need more than an eyelash—or dust from the ground—to make new human beings. This is the same God who fed over 5,000 people with only five loaves of bread and two fish, even though the fish were not alive. Since John 5:17 states that God continues to work even on the Sabbath, it is within reason that He could have resumed creating men and women on what might be considered an *eighth day*.

Seeing humanity's shared origin—whether from a single act of creation or an ongoing creative process—ties all these themes together and returns us to the central message of God's vast purpose and love.

Every question about early humanity ultimately circles back to the same focal point: God's overarching plan and endless love. Whether God created additional people alongside Adam and Eve or repopulated the earth in ways beyond human comprehension, the central message is one of divine purpose. As with Conversation One, the challenge is to remain open to Scripture's broader possibilities while keeping the Creator's intent in mind. Let each insight inspire a deeper relationship with the Lord who made us, sustains us, and calls us into fellowship through His unchanging love and sovereign design.

GIVING U.P.
Thoughts

Conversation Three
EVE AND ADAM'S FALL
Is the pursuit of knowledge good or bad?

Most people would tell you that knowledge is power, and they would be right! As long as you know how to use that knowledge effectively there is power. However, it would help if you always considered the cost of knowledge. Adam and Eve did not fully understand or know the price they would have to pay for the knowledge they gained. If they did, maybe they could have avoided the fall. Let's dive deeper into the story of the Fall of Eve and Adam. There are a few lessons and different perspectives, rarely discussed, we can take away from the story of the first man and woman's fall.

The first perspective is from the timeline of Eve and Adam eating the fruit. As you may have noticed in the previous paragraph, I wrote Eve first, then Adam, when referring to their fall. I did this intentionally. Eve consumed the fruit from the tree of the knowledge of good and evil first, and then gave the fruit to Adam to eat. Time and order of events should always be considered and weighed for importance when reading the Bible. Eve ate the fruit first. Therefore, one can assume she felt/knew the pain of shame and regret first.

A question one can ask to gain perspective is, when did Eve start to feel the effects of the fruit? Was she already feeling shame and regret before or as she was giving the fruit to Adam and still decided to give it to him to eat? If Eve knew and still gave Adam the fruit, did she deceive Adam about the effects of what she felt? I believe that if she did feel the pain of shame and regret and still gave the fruit to Adam, she didn't do it because she didn't love Adam. She loved Adam. Eve gave the fruit to Adam for two possible distinct reasons.

EVE'S REASONS

First, Eve became aware of humanity's possibilities, limitations, and power. Maybe Eve wanted to leverage this newfound knowledge and persuade Adam to achieve her newfound will and desires. Could Eve's first desire after gaining knowledge have been to control her husband? If this were the case, then maybe Eve's thinking would explain why one of God's punishments for women was that their husbands would rule over them, even though they would desire to rule them (Genesis 3:16).

The second plausible reason for Eve giving Adam the fruit, even though she felt the outcome of eating it, is she got a quick idea of what loneliness felt like. Also, she felt her mortality for the first time and didn't want to experience life and death alone.

Understand that those two got a rush of knowledge all at once, and with that knowledge came emotions they might not have known how to handle. Imagine feeling shame, regret, confusion, and loss all at once for the first time. Think about the timeline of her eating first, then giving the fruit to Adam. I am not saying Eve had to feel this way, but it is a possibility to consider.

AFTER EATING THE BITTER(SWEET) FRUIT

The second perspective from which to view the story of the fall is the change in Eve and Adam after consuming the fruit from the tree of knowledge of good and evil. There was an immediate change in both Eve and Adam. The Bible says their eyes were open, and they suddenly realized their nakedness. After Eve and Adam consumed the fruit, their intellectual makeup changed. Once God addressed their sin, their physical makeup, cultural relationships, and environmental surroundings changed. From this story, we see that when humans sin, disobedience affects us mentally, emotionally, intellectually, physically, culturally, and environmentally. Not only does it affect us, but it also affects our children and others around us, but that is another discussion.

One can theorize that Adam and Eve were created equally, physically, and intellectually. Although they were different in several ways, such as male and female, they were equal partners in their relationship. God addressed the man (Adam) when dealing with issues (Genesis 3:9) because He created Adam first and verbally gave him the laws to uphold. An example of this is God speaking with Moses instead of the entire nation of Israel. God gave the commandments and statutes to Moses, so he addressed Moses when the people sinned. Even with God addressing Adam first, Adam and Eve were still equal partners in their relationship (Gen 2:18, 23-25). The Bible says Eve was suitable for Adam (v. 18). She was from his rib, had the same flesh and bone (v. 23), and had similar DNA. They were one flesh. In other words, they were equal not only physically but in thought and shared emotions, desires, and needs (v. 24). They were both naked and felt no shame (v. 25). Consider them as equals because when they looked at each other and walked around the Garden, together or apart, there was nothing between them that they could see that made them feel less than, greater than, or inadequate. They were in complete oneness with their partner.

After they ate the fruit and before the LORD addressed them, they changed mentally and emotionally. Their bodies didn't change physically at this point, but they simultaneously felt the need to cover up. They felt shame over their bodies, which had not changed. They hid their bodies from each other. Remember, they were made from the same DNA. They knew they were from the same flesh (v. 23). There was no reason for them to hide or feel ashamed about the body they had. There was no one else there to hide their bodies from except for the other. They hid their bodies from each other, as well as God. Before their sin, there was no reason for shame because they were equal. So, we see from their actions that your sin can instantly change your way of thinking, seeing, and feeling.

THE FRUIT'S COSMETIC PROPERTIES

After God addressed their sin, Eve's physical makeup changed, and her cultural relationship with her mate shifted in responsibility. Before the fall, God's intent was for women to have children pain-free. After the fall, childbirth brought tears, screams, c-sections, scars, stretch marks, and more. Before the fall, God intended for women and men to be equal partners, sharing responsibilities. After, God said the man will rule over you (Gen 3:16).

What is one way a man can (maybe not always) establish dominance over a woman? Physical strength. Therefore, one can assume that when God changed a woman's body to experience pain in childbirth, He changed it in physical strength as well. Since they shared responsibilities in the Garden, one can deduce that Eve, who felt no shame, could conduct all the same tasks Adam could, such as cultivating the Garden and working with animals.

When God addressed Adam, He made no mention of physical adjustments. Adam's punishment came in the form of work and toil. Humankind would have to work and work hard to eat. This work impacts his daily walk with God and thus his daily experience of feeling fulfillment throughout the day. Before the fall, all Adam had to do was enjoy his wife and walk with God. Afterward, he would have to leave his wife to work in a field and focus on doing the necessary things to eat and clothe himself and his family. This focus on the painstaking work took his focus away from God. This environmental change would change his life physically, mentally, emotionally, culturally, and, most of all, spiritually.

Note: Remember, not all men and women are equal physically, mentally, and intellectually. Therefore, roles and responsibilities within relationships will differ from the next man's, woman's, or household's interconnection. So do not look at your neighbor and compare your relationship or roles within the household with their relationship and roles within their household. They can and likely will be different.

THE SHAME OF KNOWLEDGE

One thing I want to meditate on and sit on is the eye-opening revelation Eve and Adam received all at once. As stated earlier, after eating the fruit, a rush of information, knowledge, and images flooded their minds. I would go so far as to say that Adam and Eve experienced the greatest shame and grief that anyone has ever experienced.

Why do I say that? Think about it like this. When we mature and learn tough lessons, we normally do that in stages or during isolated events in our lives. A young child learns not to touch the stove at one isolated event, which was the only lesson they learned at that time. Then, that same child learns that not staying balanced on the bike can lead to some pain. A teenager learns the lesson or pain of a breakup. When we learn our lessons on good and evil or pain and obedience, we learn it in stages over time. To some extent, as we learn each lesson, we are allowed time to cope with that one lesson before facing another life lesson.

Now, think about how much Eve and Adam learned at that moment of eating the fruit and try to imagine the multitude of knowledge they had at once. Think about the loss of innocence they had in that moment. Now, think about the emotions and having to deal with that moment. They had a lifetime of life lessons that they were baptized with and the pain of shame and guilt that went along with it.

The realization that they were naked was not the only thing they learned at that moment. It was the only thing that the author addressed. They dealt with the shame of their bodies. They dealt with the fear of disobedience. They discovered all the differences between good and evil at that moment.

Understand, it was the tree of the knowledge of good and evil. In each fruit, in each bite of the fruit, there was a wealth of knowledge on the possibilities of all the good and evil this world is capable of, but no understanding of God's forgiveness, mercy, and love. Think about that. To understand God's love and mercy, one must experience it. They must see it and feel it. Before eating the fruit, there was no reason for shame or experiencing God's mercy. Eve and Adam, in those moments after they ate the fruit, must have felt a level of shame that no one has experienced since.

EVERY BITE COUNTS

So, what does this perspective give you? How can you look at the story of Adam and Eve and glean an understanding that can help you today? First, let's revisit the perspective of timing. Although Eve ate first, Adam saw nothing in her or the surrounding area that stopped him from eating the fruit. We learn that someone can be in the act of disobedience and sin, and everything looks fine for that person. Someone could be actively sinning and ask you to join them (not necessarily with the intent of hurting you), and no consequences or repercussions will occur until you are in the mix of sin with them.

Well, you may say, Adam was there with Eve. Yes, he was eventually beside her by the tree, but he was not present for Eve and the serpent's entire conversation. Genesis 3:13 and 2 Corinthians 11:3 state that Eve was deceived, not Eve and Adam. Adam was not tricked or misled by the serpent's words. Therefore, he may not have exchanged words with the serpent before eating the fruit. We know that Eve spoke with the serpent, decided of her own volition to eat the fruit, and then gave the fruit to Adam. Adam chose to eat with his wife. No one forced him.

The timing of their actions aligned so that neither understood the full ramifications of their sin until after both ate the fruit of the tree of knowledge of good and evil. We can take this away: just because you see someone getting away with something you know is wrong doesn't mean you will get away with it if you join them. Also, the consequences of disobedient actions may not be felt immediately, but the pain can be overwhelming when the consequences come.

GROWING PAINS AND LESSONS LEARNED

Not only can the pain resulting from our actions be overwhelming, but we also learned that it could affect us in many ways. When the LORD passed down the punishment on Eve and Adam, it affected them in multiple ways. Eve and Adam's life changed physically, emotionally, intellectually, culturally, socially, and spiritually. Not only did it affect them personally, but it also affected their surroundings and the lives of generations to come.

We not only see how sin entered the world, but we also see how sin and the deception leading to our sin can affect us today. When reading the Bible, we should ask ourselves if there is an unfamiliar perspective from which this story or information can be viewed. Once you start looking at the Bible from various points of view, you can see that there can be a greater understanding or a different lesson than the one received at church. God has many ways that He draws near to us. Don't limit yourself or put our God in a box that only allows for minimal or narrow perspectives to reveal His love, truth, and understanding.

There is one more thing I want you to take away, as this is probably the most important lesson. When Christ is on the cross, He cries out to God and asks, *"Why have you forsaken me?"* (Matthew 27:46 and Mark 15:34). Now, think back to that rush of shame and guilt Eve and Adam felt after they ate the fruit from the tree. That's what the Lord felt throughout His entire process of sacrifice. The pain He felt from the sin of the world started with the beatings, whipping, and lashing. It remained upon Him during the march to the hill of Golgotha with the cross on His back, through the nailing of His body on the cross, and until His death. The shame and grief of our sins rushed upon him long before He was nailed to the cross. Now, think about that. The same rush of pain that Eve and Adam felt from their sin is the same overwhelming pain Christ felt throughout His last hours alive. So, when you think that the Lord doesn't know how you feel when you are going through an addiction or experiencing the shame of your mistakes, think again. He knows. He feels for you and loves you more than you know.

Conversation Four

THE BLESSING OF ABRAHAM

Are children a blessing?

Have children always been regarded as a blessing, or does Scripture point to a deeper meaning behind God's promise to make someone fruitful? Have you ever looked at a drawing of something and needed clarification on what it was? It is easy to misunderstand things because everyone sees things from different perspectives. That's why we must stop and revisit certain notions since, often, we can miss the point at first glance. There are events in the Bible we should revisit and look at in a new light, such as the blessing bestowed upon Abraham.

Many people misunderstand the blessing of Abraham (Genesis 15). The blessing of Abraham (Abram) had to include his wife, Sarah (Sarai). The blessing was not only for Abraham alone. Because of that, we can conclude that the blessing was not merely being able to conceive a child. If it was for Abraham alone and just being able to have a child,

Abraham would have already been blessed with the birth of Ishmael through Hagar.

Thus, the blessing was, and is, what children can bring to both parents. It is a greater understanding of who God is and how He sees us (His children). More specifically, it is a greater understanding of His love, patience, grace, and mercy. This understanding is only achieved through maintaining a relationship with Him through the various situations experienced in one's lifetime.

Many misunderstand this blessing. People believe that the blessing was the child, Isaac. However, Isaac merely presented the opportunity for the blessing to be received. Isaac was not the blessing himself. There is so much more to it.

THE BLESSING IN PARENTHOOD

Anyone who has raised or is raising a child knows that a child in and of themselves is not a blessing. They can get on your nerves. They can bring pain, frustration, and weariness. They can bring 18+ years of demanding responsibility and financial burden. Real parents know that the responsibility of raising a child does not end when they graduate high school or go to college. Real parents know that parenting and helping our children ends when you pass away.

Understand that the blessing is not just to those who can conceive a child. The blessing includes parents of adopted children, foster children, aunts, uncles, and those who assume the guardianship role. The blessing is for those who commit to raising a child, from the child's start to the guardian's finish, in the way they should go--the way our Lord and Savior would want them to be raised. That is who the blessing is for. It is not for those who raise a child in a manner that is not pleasing to the Lord.

The blessing is raising the child while leaning on the Lord and gaining His perspective throughout the entire process. We all know that our learning and maturity process continues until the day we pass from this Earth. The blessing that comes with raising a child is sustainable as parents are making a continued commitment to raising a child in a manner that is pleasing to the Lord, a manner that keeps His name honored and glorified throughout generations. The blessing is not a one-time gift. It is a gift that is given and received whenever we choose to go to the well.

What is the well? The well is prayer and a walk with the Lord. Yes, it is that simple. Through prayer and a relationship with our Lord, we gain wisdom and understanding when we ask and sometimes when we don't know to ask. This wisdom and understanding are the central part of the blessing God wanted to give Abraham and Sarah. God wanted to give Abraham, Sarah, and their descendants a blessing to improve their relationship with Him and honor and glorify Himself for generations.

Other material blessings can come with having children. But that is not what God was doing with Isaac. Abraham and Sarah were already blessed materially. They had possessions, land, and servants. They didn't need more of that. They were not asking for or needed more of that. Abraham, Sarah, and their descendants needed a greater understanding of their

God. They needed a greater understanding of His power, love, grace, and mercy. They did not have that. Sarai laughed when she heard that she would be having a child. Why? Because she didn't have a good understanding of God's power and love. She gained a greater idea of that through the conception, birth, and raising of Isaac.

UNLOCK THE BLESSING

Children, alone, are not a blessing. They present the opportunity of a blessing from the perspective God gives you as you walk with Him throughout your child-raising process. In addition to the love and, in some cases, assistance children can give, children can be a means for parents to learn more about God and themselves as parents and maturing adults. Having kids puts you into the game, a different game than those that are single. Raising them allows you to earn points (favor), abilities (gifts or talents like wisdom and patience), or treasures (eternal rewards one receives in Heaven) that only the Lord can give. You still earn these things when you are single, but the Lord gives you an additional path to earning rewards when you have children. It is like having a different credit card that stretches your limit and gives you extra opportunities to earn points or rewards.

As we raise children and walk with the Lord, we learn about ourselves and how God sees us. Based on that, we grow or pass the levels of the game and earn. We don't reach the next level of *the game* until we understand the point God wants us to see. We find ourselves stuck on the same level, revisiting the same problems, with our kids because we have not yet figured out all God wants us to learn. Sometimes, that same lesson we are trying to instill in our kids is the same lesson God is trying to show us as adults. The Lord tells us that our adult actions and thinking are the same way our child thinks.

Although we grow older, our selfish, childlike way of thinking sometimes doesn't change. We just want more adult-oriented objects, whereas our children want more child-oriented objects of enjoyment.

GIFTS AND REWARDS

To fully grasp the topic, you have to shift your perspective. Think of children as a gift and reward in terms of the covenant God made with Abraham. First, think about what the Lord ultimately (eternally) wants for you. Focus on eternity, not just the earthly will God planned for you. Then, think about growing old on Earth and how children can make that better.

I want to look at Psalm 127. In the original text of this chapter, Solomon talks about the blessing of a son. He specifically mentions sons, but this same outlook should also be tied to daughters.

> *Unless the Lord builds the house, the builders labor in vain. Unless the Lord watches over the city, the guards stand watch in vain. In vain you rise early and stay up late, toiling for food to eat—for He grants sleep to those He loves. Children are a provision/heritage from the Lord, offspring, a reward from Him. Like arrows in the hands of a warrior are children born in one's youth. Blessed is the man whose quiver is full of them. They will not be put to shame when they contend with their opponents in court.*
>
> **PSALM 127:1-5 (NIV)**

REWARD VERSUS GIFT

A *reward* is something given in return for some completed act. A *gift* is something voluntarily transferred without compensation. In other words, a gift is something that one can receive without earning it. One can receive a gift out of pure love from the giver for the recipient. A gift is expressed as a provision or heritage in the Hebrew text.

Provision is a supply or requirement of something. A provision fulfills a need before the need is needed. It is provided by being prepared beforehand. Remember the old game Oregon Trail. The player would get their provisions before they set out on the trail.

Heritage is expressed as a legacy or inheritance. A heritage can be someone you can pass something down to, someone who continues to magnify your name and traditions. Along with this discussion of heritage and gifts is the term birthright. A birthright is an inheritance that can be a gift, a reward, or both.

When you represent someone's name, you represent their nature (birthright in the form of a gift) and their character (birthright in the form of a reward). Also, you represent their legacy, the fruit of heritage.

When you have a child, you are blessed with an opportunity to cultivate another disciple for the Lord, someone who reflects God's light. Along with that opportunity, you can cultivate and nurture someone who will continue representing your nature, legacy, and name. They can continue along your path, the path with the Lord. Although their path with the Lord is uniquely set for them, it is the same path of righteousness you chose to walk.

The Lord wanted us to make disciples (Matthew 28:19). Children are a gift, starting as a blank slate to mold little Christians (disciples) who will earn you rewards in Heaven. This concept brings me back to Psalm 127:1. As a parent or guardian, you can lay the foundation of discipleship for that child, with Christ as the builder. If the Lord is not the foundation of that child's upbringing, you will be working long hours trying to raise a *good person* in vain.

Understand that a blessing is meant for more than just the primary recipient(s) of the blessing. It is intended for others. Your gift (blessing) of being one of the saved, *the called to Christ,* is meant for you to relay that call to others. So, the lessons you learned through your trials should help others through their trials while making or strengthening disciples in the process. The lessons your children learn should help the next generation through its trials while making disciples in the process. You are paying it forward to future generations, but that future fruit you are sewing into now is credited to your account in Heaven.

There is so much more to this story of Abraham, Sarah, and Isaac. However, the main point is that the process of raising a child, with a focus on pleasing God and maintaining a relationship with God throughout the process, opens you up to blessings. Don't let the gift of conceiving or being able to conceive a child overshadow the greater blessing that God has for you. That blessing is greater wisdom and understanding through a deeper relationship with God.

GIVING U.P.
Thoughts

Conversation Five
THE WILDERNESS

Could seasons of wandering actually be periods of spiritual preparation?

When you cook a meal, do you take the time to do prep work first? It takes much more effort to prep before cooking a meal, but that extra time makes all the difference. If you don't prep, you might forget to add a particular spice or seasoning to your dish. Without that added flavor, the meal could fall flat. Like food, sometimes we need more preparation to get us just right. God does this with us often. Take the children of Israel, for example.

After the Israelites left Egypt, they were in the wilderness for forty years before they entered the Promised Land. The forty years was a period of preparation for the Israelites entering the Promised Land. Before entering the land of milk and honey, they needed to know how to operate within their promise. This message is important to us as believers and daily followers of Christ because our life on Earth is the wilderness before our promised life in Heaven. Take a second and meditate on that. Our life here on Earth is preparation for our eternal life in Heaven.

MISREPRESENTED PREPARATION

Now, I know and understand the forty years was a punishment for some. Some elders who tested and did not trust the LORD had to die off before the people could enter the Promised Land (Numbers 13-14; verses specifically on the forty years is Num 14:33-35). But the wilderness was not a punishment, or what some may consider a living purgatory, for those that would enter the promise. It was only a punishment for those who would not enter the Promised Land.

God wanted to kill all the people of Israel. But God spared Joshua, Caleb, and the rest of Israel for His own name, the sake of the people, and the development of the younger generation that could not fend for and govern themselves. The ten spies who did not trust the LORD, who turned the rest of the elders' hearts away from taking the Promised Land, died immediately. Their punishment for turning the people's hearts away from entering the Land the LORD promised them was swift. Joshua and Caleb were the only two spies who did not die because they maintained their faith in God and wanted to take the Land immediately. They believed they could conquer any obstacle since God was on their side. Since they believed, God spared them and the younger generation that did not die in the wilderness.

THE FORTY-YEAR PREP

Some may argue that forty years was a punishment for Joshua and Caleb. There is a good argument for that, but the forty years helped prepare them and helped them prepare their people for taking God's promise. For all those that would enter the Promised Land, that time in the wilderness trained them for living within their ultimate dwelling place here on Earth.

In the wilderness, the people that would eventually take possession of the Promised Land learned about the LORD. Scholars believe there were about 37 to 38 years between when the LORD established the forty-year curse and when they crossed the Jordan. During this time, the younger generation that would lead Israel into the land learned the LORD's commandments, statutes, and His power and love. Even though they witnessed it in Egypt, the next generation, which would eventually enter and take possession of the Promised Land, needed reminders. Several of them were young in Egypt and did not fully comprehend what God did for them in Egypt. They needed to witness God's awesomeness and discipline in the wilderness.

The people of Israel had to learn to operate under the laws God established for them, which they learned from Moses. They did not have their own established form of government in Egypt. The Egyptian government was their government. Moses and Aaron, the leaders that brought them out of Egypt, did not know how to run a nation of people. Remember, Moses' father-in-law, Jethro, had to show him how to establish groups of leaders among the people. This process of governing the people, told to Moses by Jethro, would eventually become Israel's form of a judicial system (Exodus 18).

After the events with the spies and the LORD deciding to delay their entry into the Promised Land for forty years, Israel still received more laws from Moses and experienced trials, plagues, and opposition. The Israelites received laws on sojourners, giving offerings, handling dead bodies, cities of refuge, and inheritance for women. They experienced the anger and power of God through the ordeals with Korah's rebellion, the serpents, and the plague. Israel experienced God's love through their success in war with the Amorite Kings and the Midianites. They did not lose a single man during the battle with the Midianites. The Levitical priest received guidance on their duties and their cities. Moses passed down how the land would be parceled amongst the families. Most importantly, Joshua was named Moses' successor. Through these experiences, the next generation learned a great deal because of their period of waiting, which better prepared them for entering the Promised Land.

MATURING IN THE IN-BETWEEN

So, why is it vital for us as believers and followers of Christ to know that there was a period of growth and development between leaving Egypt and entering the land of promise? We need to understand that when we become believers and are set free from the devil's bondage, this is just the beginning. Some of us may get to the Promised Land

(Heaven) sooner than others after we accept Christ as our Savior. But all of us have growth and development that the LORD wants to take place between our acceptance of Christ and our ascension to Heaven.

This process of preparation, growth, and development is what theologians call progressive sanctification and what the Bible calls walking in the Spirit. The New Testament talks about working toward spiritual maturity and becoming more Christlike. We are not expected to be perfect as soon as we are freed from the shackles of sin. There is no example of a perfect person in the Bible except for Jesus Christ. Elijah, Elisha, Job, John the Baptist, and Mary (pick any Mary in the Bible) all stumbled in their walk. Everyone, after they become saved, requires growth.

Christ understands we will still stumble after we accept Him as our savior. The LORD knows we still require growth as believers. After walking with Christ for three and a half years, even the disciples failed to hit the mark on various occasions. In John 14, Jesus told the disciples that after He returned to Heaven, He would send them a Helper, an Advocate, to help them in their walk of discipleship. This Helper is the Holy Spirit. The Holy Spirit's job is to guide us through the wilderness while we wait to be called to our modern-day Promised Land (Heaven). Another job of the Holy Spirit is to reveal wisdom at the right time to believers to aid in our growth and development.

THE WAY OUT OF THE WILDERNESS

You are probably asking, *"Why is my spiritual growth important for my eternal life in Heaven?"* God is a God of order. He is the King in the kingdom of Heaven. In that kingdom, there is a system of operation. Heaven is not a place where people are floating on clouds, playing harps throughout eternity. The Bible tells us that there are distinct roles and responsibilities within the heavenly kingdom that require obedience and order. Similarly, once the Israelites entered the Promised Land, their daily life and operations would require them to maintain a level of obedience and order.

God gave Moses the commandments, laws, and statutes for the nation of Israel to obey once they entered their promise. If they did not do this, there would be disorder and chaos within the land. The laws God gave Moses differed from those they had to follow in Egypt. Furthermore, they were different than the laws of every other nation and kingdom on Earth. The Bible states that God wanted the people of Israel to be different than every other group of people on Earth. The LORD wanted them to carry themselves differently from all other people.

As believers and followers of Christ, we are preparing ourselves to operate in a place different from any other place on Earth. We will live in a kingdom with more order and peace than any kingdom that ever reigned on Earth. For us to maintain the order required of the citizens of Heaven, our spirits must have some level of Christlike maturity.

Thus, I believe that the LORD may recycle underdeveloped souls so they may be allowed an opportunity to develop into more mature Christlike beings. Trust in His process. Prepare yourself in the interim. God has plans for us; if we move according to His will, we know the destination will be worthwhile.

GIVING U.P.

Conversation Six

GOD'S LOVE AND THE POINT OF SOUL DEVELOPMENT

Is there a purpose to the underdeveloped soul?

Have you ever wondered how even a life cut short might still carry the promise of divine growth and eternal purpose? In this conversation, I examine a question that has long intrigued me: How can a soul, no matter how brief its earthly experience, fully encounter and reflect God's love? My exploration is personal and rooted in Scripture, inviting you to consider whether the process of soul development—even for those souls that seem underdeveloped—reveals the boundless mercy and creative power of our God.

As stated in the beginning, one's thinking when reading this and thinking about this world, humanity, and purpose—it all starts, revolves around, and ends with God's love. Paul's desire and prayer for the church at Ephesus is rooted in God's desire for His people:

> *For this reason I bow my knees before the Father, from whom every family in heaven and on earth derives its name, that He would*

grant you, according to the riches of His glory, to be strengthened with power through His Spirit in the inner man, so that Christ may dwell in your hearts through faith; and that you, being rooted and grounded in love, may be able to comprehend with all the saints what is the breadth and length and height and depth, 19and to know the love of Christ which surpasses knowledge, that you may be filled up to all that fullness of God. Now to Him who is able to do far more abundantly beyond all that we ask or think, according to the power that works within us, to Him be the glory in the church and in Christ Jesus to all generations forever and ever. Amen.

EPHESIANS 3:14-21 (NASB)

Keep this in mind as we go through this next section. One of God's desires for all His souls is to know the love of Christ. Also, remember that God can do more than we ask or think.

Throughout this next topic discussion, there are questions meant for you to consider a new perspective. You do not have to accept my opinion but rather think of an unfamiliar perspective other than what you may have been given or hold.

There is an old Christian creed that says, *"The chief end of man is to know (glorify) God and enjoy Him forever."* Ask yourself this question: How can a soul whose life has been cut short in its infant or preadolescent years know, glorify, or enjoy God? To put the question another way, how can that soul understand its eternal resting place if it never got an opportunity to understand who it is and why it is where it is? This brings me to my next topic, the underdeveloped soul, and how it relates to God's control and management of souls.

THE DEFINITION OF AN UNDERDEVELOPED SOUL

My definition will differ from other definitions. For example, in his book Letters to a Young Doctor, Richard Selzer describes a few doctors he knows as arrogant and overbearing. Selzer says, *"They own underdeveloped souls, the blighted wisps having slipped into their perfect frames at the moment of birth to live out their tenancy unacknowledged."* The doctor's words and description of underdeveloped souls are very well stated.

Here is why my definition differs. I would call an arrogant and overbearing adult who has lived life long enough to earn their doctorate and work as a surgeon a developed soul—an inward-looking developed soul, one that has molded and defined values, principles, and goals to revolve around self-gratification and self-glorification.

For the sake of the following discussion, an underdeveloped soul is one that has not had the opportunity to understand what their soul is. Also, it does not understand the significance of a purpose or higher calling in their life. Underdeveloped souls never had the opportunity to try and define themselves or seek meaning for their lives, whether that meaning is through God, some other perceived higher power, or some other area or thing in our universe.

UNDERSTANDING THE NEED FOR DEVELOPMENT

Let's go back and meditate on the old Christian creed, *"To know or to glorify God and to enjoy Him forever."* First, to know something or someone, one must learn, be taught, or be introduced to that something or someone. Second, to glorify anything or anyone, one must learn or be taught how to glorify it. Third, to enjoy God forever means not only to enjoy the Lord God here on earth but also in heaven. Therefore, we must learn what heaven and forever entail or require of us before we get there to enjoy it fully. All humans with a soul should not only be focused on their earthly end in enjoying God but also their eternal forever with God in heaven.

It is safe to say that part of why we are on earth is to develop our souls for our eternal dwelling. My mother once said, *"God could've made all of us adults at our creation, but He didn't."* The point my mother was making is that we (her children) had a lot to learn before we questioned her or my dad or before we thought we were grown. She was saying there is something to our growth process that is important to our earthly and eternal life. Whether the process is being brought up or bringing up another person, there is something about growth and development that is important and must not be ignored.

CAN AN UNDERDEVELOPED SOUL FIND PURPOSE IN ETERNITY?

If an underdeveloped soul is separated from its earthly dwelling (body), its chief end is not experienced. This can also be said of a lot of believers and nonbelievers who are adults. But for those where the preparation process is never started—those souls whose development never got a chance to take root spiritually—what happens to them? What knowledge of Christ and the processes of heaven did they learn or get introduced to? What treasures did they have an opportunity to earn (Matthew 6:19–20)? If there is no marriage in heaven and no need for gender/sex identification, nor the development or upbringing of children (Matthew 22:30), and we all are *"like angels,"* then what happens to all the souls taken at a young earthly age?

Billy Graham once said, *"It is during our lifetime here on earth that we decide our eternal destiny."* The key word in that statement is *decide*. It is through our decisions that we decide if and how we know God, glorify God, and enjoy God. What decision does an underdeveloped soul intelligently make?

GOD'S CHARACTER AND BIBLICAL EXAMPLES

Attention now shifts to God's makeup and character, still pertinent to the discussion. When the Israelites went into Jericho, they were instructed to kill every man, woman, and child, and they did so (Deuteronomy 20:16; Joshua 6:21). Then, around the time of Jesus's birth, Herod ordered the killing of all male babies under the age of two (Matthew 2:16). There are also mass killings of infants and preadolescents recorded in Egypt in the book of Exodus. One thing to note is that God commanded Moses and Joshua to kill the people of Jericho.

The Bible tells us that God is holy (Leviticus 11:44; 1 Samuel 2:2), righteous (Psalms 11:7), without sin (1 John 3:5), and He cannot tell someone to sin. Charles C. Ryrie (1925–2016), Bible scholar and theologian, described God's holiness and righteousness in this way: *"In respect to God, holiness means not only that He is separate from all that is unclean and evil but also that He is positively pure and thus distinct from all others*" (Basic Theology, page 42). "*Holiness relates to God's separateness, righteousness, to His justice. Righteousness has to do with law, morality, and justice... there is no law, either within His own being or of His own making, that is violated by anything in His nature... there is no action He takes that violates any code of morality or justice.*" (Basic Theology, page 48)

Therefore, when we see the commandment from God to execute and end the earthly life of not only adults but also children in the Bible, there had to be a deeper purpose. The order had to be part of a bigger plan by God. His character would not allow for the senseless and pointless ending of innocent, underdeveloped souls. Keep this in mind as you continue to read.

So, are we to think that these underdeveloped souls, these spiritually and morally immature souls, are in heaven? The Bible tells us they are. Then what is their purpose or responsibility in heaven? What is the point of our chief end here on earth?

A SECOND CHANCE

These souls never got an opportunity to fully understand Christ's love. Nor did they get opportunities to earn treasures here on earth or learn how treasures impact one's eternal experience in heaven. If they get the opportunity in heaven, what would that process entail? Why would or should one take the process of learning the fullness and love of Christ and earning treasures seriously on earth if there is an opportunity later in heaven?

One might say God grants the opportunity to earn treasures in heaven to those who died in infancy or preadolescence. Another argument one can offer is that they did not hear about the Lord or His teachings until late in life or right before they died. What will their opportunity to earn treasures entail?

One option I would like you to consider is that God joins underdeveloped souls with new bodies. We have seen evidence that God can create new souls, more people. Now, consider that He gives these underdeveloped souls a new opportunity through a second or however many chances He chooses to give a soul to accept His love. These are the souls that never got the opportunity in one body to develop and define who or what they wanted to be and who or what they wanted to serve. If we had the opportunity to define ourselves in heaven without error, then there would be no need for earth.

A DIFFERENT VIEW

Plato and other Greek philosophers held a view of preexistence. Preexistence revolved around the idea that, at the beginning, God created all human souls, which were confined in physical bodies as punishment (Basic Theology, page 221). This view goes against Biblical teachings of God's holiness and righteousness. If God is a just God, he would not create a soul with the intent of punishing it without cause. Preexistence thinking goes on to state that souls go through various incarnations throughout time and incur sinfulness. It is not hard to understand or believe that God may give certain souls, or all souls, opportunities to hear, see, and feel God's love, to know Christ's love, and be given a chance to love Him back through another chance or various *incarnations*. However, I do not believe the soul incurs or stacks up sinfulness through the given opportunities of incarnation. 1 Corinthians 13:5 says love *"does not take into account a wrong suffered,"* therefore incurring or stacking up sins to be judged upon later is something I do not agree with.

When a child is taken away from their bodies during an infantile or preadolescent stage, the point of that may be to serve some purpose to draw another individual into an opportunity to define their life and draw themselves closer or farther away from God. It serves as a test for an adult or mature individual or to put an individual through a situation to serve as a testimony and a guide to another individual who may go through the same thing, which in turn draws that person(s) to God or away from God; and more importantly, presents the opportunity for one to choose to glorify or even curse God.

I understand this topic may touch deeper for some, and I do not want to sound inconsiderate of their experiences. Losing a child of any age is something that is difficult to live with, so I apologize if this hurts someone. I just want you to consider that the child may get another chance. If they do not get another chance, then they are in heaven waiting to see you again.

When David lost his first child with Bathsheba, his servant asked him why he stopped fasting and weeping to eat—because most people at that time fasted after they lost a loved one. David knew that there was a life beyond this one we have on earth. David told his servant that he would go to his child (2 Samuel 12:23). In other words, David said he would see his child in heaven, so he did not have to mourn anymore.

Someone will read this and say, *"There you go. Children go to heaven."* I totally agree with you, as I stated earlier. The souls of children go to heaven. I am not arguing that; I am saying that for the underdeveloped souls, like David's child, God can send them back into bodies to get their chance at developing and defining who they are. Those who accept the love of God will all know and see our families in new heavenly bodies.

One thing to note: how we look here on earth will not be how we look in heaven. Just as God put knowledge and intelligence in Adam and Eve, He can impart that same knowledge of who our family and friends are once we get to heaven in our eternal bodies. Once in the afterlife—whether in heaven or hell—we will recognize or know the soul, not merely the physical body that we once knew or recognized.

I know I deviated a bit, but I return now to my previous discussion point of the underdeveloped soul being given another opportunity. The underdeveloped soul has another opportunity without knowledge of its previous life—either to be used by God in the same manner as before or to be given a chance to fully develop and define itself without the influence of prior incarnations. The soul is ultimately judged based on the decisions it makes during its full opportunity to mature, develop, and define itself.

THE POWER TO DEFINE AND OUR UNIQUENESS AS HUMANS

This ability to define is critical to understanding the purpose and uniqueness of humankind. When God created humanity, He said His creation was *"very good."* With all the other creations, He saw that it was good; it was not until He created both man and woman that His entire creation was deemed *"very good."*

Consider what separated us from the other creations. What separated humans from animals, beasts, fish, birds, and nature? It is not our ability to communicate with God or for God to communicate with us—because we see passages in the Bible where God communicates with animals and nature. God commanded the large fish to swallow Jonah. He directed the animals to go to Noah's Ark. Jesus commanded the waves and the wind to be still (Mark 4:39). Also, it is not merely our ability to praise and worship, as 1 Chronicles 16:32–33, Isaiah 55:12, and Revelation 5:13 tell us that nature and every creature can make noises and sing praises, with Jesus even telling us in Luke 19:40 that stones can cry out in praise.

So, what separates us and makes us *"very good?"* It is our ability to define, choose, and decide what things—including ourselves—will be. The sun is the sun and can do nothing else but be the sun. The trees, although capable of praise, cannot define what something else is. Although beautiful and unique, it is the natural God-directed process for the caterpillar to become a butterfly. Animals can feel pain, show emotion, think, and even decide on a path, but an animal cannot define or change being that animal or the process of becoming that animal.

Humans have the ability—with our words and actions—to define a beast, a tool, or the character of an animal or individual. This was the ultimate defining moment of creation. This defining ability, bestowed upon us, is what gave us our power to rule over and subdue the earth and all that is in it. This power is what is *"very good."* This power is also what God judges when placing us in our eternal dwelling place.

How we use our power to define ourselves is what will be judged—and it is this power that underdeveloped souls do not get to consciously exercise. If not given another chance, then they cannot exercise the power to mature, develop, and define who they will be, whom or what they will glorify, and who or what they will enjoy.

God's judgment is also important to understand in this discussion on underdeveloped souls. Romans 2:11–16 outlines our Lord's judgment of all believers and nonbelievers:

For there is no partiality with God. For all who have sinned without the Law will also perish without the Law and all who have sinned under the Law will be judged by the Law; for it is not the hearers of the Law who are just before God, but the doers of the Law will be justified. For when Gentiles who do not have the Law do instinctively the things of the Law, these, not having the Law, are a law to themselves, in that they show the work of the Law written in their hearts, their conscience bearing witness and their thoughts alternately accusing or else defending them, on the day when, according to my gospel, God will judge the secrets of men through Christ Jesus.

ROMANS 2:11–16

Acts 4:12 and John 14:6 should be discussed with this passage from Romans.

And there is salvation in no one else; for there is no other name under heaven that has been given among men by which we must be saved.

ACTS 4:12

Jesus said to him, 'I am the way, and the truth, and the life; no one comes to the Father but through Me.'

JOHN 14:6

These passages are clear. The verses in Romans tell us that whether one is called or not, saved or unsaved, judgment comes through Christ. Acts and John further state that the only way to be saved is through Christ.

Although Paul's reference to the Law in this Romans passage pertains to the Old Testament Mosaic Law, the judgment still applies to those who have not received the New Testament gospel. We know that at the time of Paul's writing, many people worldwide had not heard of the Mosaic Law or Christ, and the gospel did not reach them through the apostles or other disciples. So, how were they judged? They were judged by their hearts, according to Romans 2—judged by God but through Christ, as indicated in all three passages. Now apply this judgment to an underdeveloped soul: What are they being judged on?

SOUL CREATION AND GOD'S SOVEREIGN ROLE

Again, I want to remind you that this is still the same God that creates soul and body—the same God who sent the souls of the dead back into refurbished bodies after Christ's death and resurrection (Matthew 27:52–53). Can this same God not give these underdeveloped souls an opportunity to develop and define themselves and their hearts?

This power of God to create souls and unite or reunite them with the earthly body is not a new or strictly Biblical concept. The idea of preexistence—taught by Plato and other Greeks—was briefly mentioned earlier. Although not every aspect of that view is accepted, the notion that God can create souls and control their ultimate and intermediate dwellings is maintained.

Another perspective is that of Creationism. Charles Hodge, the well-known principal of Princeton Theological Seminary from 1851 to 1878, taught that Creationism holds that God creates the soul at the moment of conception or birth and immediately unites it with the body.[3] Hodge discusses mankind's sinful nature as being *inherited* through the body at birth. The purpose here is not to agree or disagree with Hodge's beliefs on Creationism but rather to affirm the thought that God creates souls and gives life to all.

Hodge cites Numbers 16:22, in which Moses and Aaron declare that God is the one who gives breath to all. He also cites Hebrews 12:9, which states that God is the Father of all spirits. [4]Additionally, Jeremiah 1:5(CSB) is introduced into

---

3[Charles Hodge, Systematic Theology (Grand Rapids: Eerdmans, 1940), 2:70ff; page 221 of Basic Theology, Charles C. Ryrie]
4 [Charles Hodge, Systematic Theology (Grand Rapids: Eerdmans, 1940), 2:70ff; page 221 of Basic Theology, Charles C. Ryrie]

the discussion: *"I chose you before I formed you in the womb; I set you apart before you were born."* The wording in the Jewish Publication Society's Tanakh—*"Before you were born, I consecrated you..."*—emphasizes that God's creation of men and women goes beyond the physical; the act of consecration includes molding the inner spirit and soul of an individual.

Jeremiah 1:5 shows that God set apart Jeremiah. This does not necessarily mean God engages in the creation of every human's soul and body as He did with Jeremiah; rather, He can be selective. He holds the power to control souls down to the minutest material and immaterial detail, as well as its ultimate placement in history.

This idea that God can be selective in His dealings with creation is not directly supported by the view of Traducianism. Traducianism is the belief that the soul is transmitted along with the body through the process of natural generation. An example of this is when an individual takes on not only the physical characteristics of their biological parents, but the character, behavioral, and emotional traits of their parents as well. In other words, the child is a material and immaterial mix of the parents. With Creationism, God joins the immaterial soul with the material body. With Traducianism, God is more laissez-faire and allows for the process of natural generation to take place.

My argument is not stating that God interjects Himself into every creation of a child (Creationism). My argument is that our God can veto natural generation (Traducianism) and set aside certain individuals for certain times and certain plans to fulfill His will at particular points and periods of time. Some can argue, to an extent, that God does control our soul placement through His providence—where He can influence two people coming together and thus influence natural generation—while others may say God can control what immaterial characteristics a child may possess, and people may point to examples where the child's immaterial traits do not reflect those of their parents. One well-known example of God's ability to influence soul development is seen in the conception, birth, and life of Christ.

One aspect of Traducianism I do not agree with is its use of the argument that the Bible supports that God rested on the seventh day of creation because His work of creation was finished, and no *fresh* acts (like creating new souls) were documented. It goes on to state that the Bible shows no evidence that the breath of life is breathed into anyone else other than Adam (Basic Theology, page 221). One reason I do not support this is because Numbers 16:22 states that God gives breath to all. This supports the argument that, in a way, God is involved through the Holy Spirit in the creation of all life.

GOD'S CREATIVE WORK DOCUMENTED

Just as the Bible does not document in detail the birth of daughters to Adam and Eve, it does not—and did not have to—document every early historical work of God. As I stated earlier, God rested on the *seventh day*, but He did not stop working. The Bible does not indicate when He started working again, but we know that He recommenced His work at some point, impacting and overseeing the lives of humanity. Is it possible for God to pick up His work on the *eighth day*? Is it possible that God breathed life into other individuals after or during Adam and Eve's stay in the Garden? The Bible did not document every single act involved with humankind after the first days of creation.

The Bible does document the power that our God has over souls. I Thessalonians 4:13–18 briefly describes Christ's second coming. Paul states that Christ will bring back to earth, with Him, the souls of those who have already died and gone to heaven. Before Jesus leaves earth again, He will raise them up to Himself first, and then the people who are still alive will be called up next. This shows the incredible power that our Lord has over our souls.

We do not see Him exercise it all the time, even though it happens every day—not in the way Paul describes, but, for example, He can bring our souls back to earth as described in 1 Thessalonians and Matthew 27:52–53, and God can take them up without them experiencing death, as in the cases of Enoch (Hebrews 11:5) and Elijah (2 Kings 2:11).

I am going to take a pause to address that this writing is not a justification to not be a disciple. I am not stating that we should not take our life, spiritual health, and growth seriously. On the contrary, we do not know how many chances we or others may get. We may be someone's best opportunity for fully understanding the love of Christ, so stay vigilant and ready. We Christians are being tested, and it was a commandment—not a suggestion—by Christ to store up treasures in heaven.

How do we do that?

We do that by being good servants, making disciples, showing the love of Christ, and bringing the knowledge of truth to others so that others may be saved. This is part of the intent and desire our God has for His people, all humanity, all His souls (Ezekiel 18:4). Passages tell us this. 1 Timothy 2:4 says our God *"desires all men to be saved and to come to the knowledge of the truth."*

Ezekiel 18:23, 32 and 2 Peter 3:9, 15 highlight another desire of our God. These verses should be discussed alongside 1 Timothy 2:4 when discussing the topic of underdeveloped souls and God's ability to move souls. Ezekiel and Peter state that God is patient with all of us and takes no pleasure in the death of anyone—specifically the eternal death of His souls. He desires His people to turn from their unrighteous ways, recognize and confess their errors, and ask God for forgiveness so that they may come to the knowledge of truth and live eternally with Him.

For the underdeveloped soul, I want to highlight 1 Timothy 2:4—the words *"to come to the knowledge of the truth"* are especially significant. The underdeveloped soul does not have the opportunity, as a developed soul has, to come to the knowledge of the truth. Now, one may ask: *What is the knowledge of truth?*

John 14:6 states that Christ, our Lord, says, *"I am the way, and the truth, and the life; no one comes to the Father but through Me."* Proverbs 1:7 and 2:6 tell us that fear of the Lord is the beginning of knowledge and that from the Lord's mouth comes knowledge and understanding. Now, some of you may be saying that even the devil and demons know who the

Lord is. Yes, this is true. The questions to ask, however, are: Do the devil and his demons fear and respect the Lord? Do they intimately know His love? Do they respect and accept His love? The answer to all those questions is no, they do not.

We can know someone but not respect or fear them or the position they may hold over us, like in a parent-child relationship. We can respect and fear someone and their position but not truly know, understand, respect, or accept their love. That is a big part of the knowledge of the truth that many of us—specifically underdeveloped souls—are missing. This love is what all the prophets and the law depend upon (Matthew 22:37–40).

Again, there is much I do not know about earth and heaven. I ask you to consider if an underdeveloped soul knows the truth and understands the basic concept(s) of love. Could this understanding come to them once they are in heaven, revealed through all the glory that surrounds them there? If that is the case, why not allow souls to have their lives cut short? Remember what my mother said: God could have made all of us adults at creation with all the knowledge our brains could hold. But there is something about the growth process—maturing, learning, growing wiser, and developing—that cannot be replaced or substituted for an underdeveloped soul.

THE ANSWERS IN EZEKIEL

Ezekiel 18 is an overlooked passage and not very well-known. Ezekiel 18 tells us that God takes no pleasure in the death of any of His children. That is an eternal death that

Ezekiel refers to. An eternal death is eternal life separated from the love and glory of God. If God desires that all developed souls come to repentance AND the knowledge of truth, then is it a reasonable question to ask, could God award underdeveloped souls and possibly those mature/developed souls that have not been introduced to the gospel of Christ another opportunity? These souls would be given an opportunity to learn about the gift that brings and comes with eternal life in heaven. With this opportunity, they could use it to decide who they are and who or what they will follow when properly introduced to the word of Christ.

In the Lord's prayer that Christ gives to His disciples in Matthew 6:9-13, Christ says something immensely powerful, *"Your will be done on earth as it is in heaven."* Our time here on earth is to learn what the will of the Father is so we can be better citizens of heaven. This is another discussion for another time, but again, this process of developing our souls for eternity [experiential/progressive sanctification (Basic Theology, page 442)] is especially important and seldom discussed.

I want to take a moment to discuss the developed souls that have not been introduced to Christ's love. In John 14:6, Jesus says, *"No one comes to the Father, except through Him."* I touched on this earlier. For some people, the law is written on their hearts, and they are judged by Christ on their willingness to allow what is written on their hearts to control their lives.

But what if their environment does not allow for that spirit inside them to be heard? We know that people, cultures, and environments can lead people away from the love of the Lord. Our families and environment can stifle the growth of the *holy* seed that is planted in all of us (Luke 8:5, 12). They can be placed behind a curtain of sin due to the actions of others and never get to receive the gift of the knowledge of Christ.

These souls need the words of the gospels. They need Christ's love to be introduced into their life, but these mature/developed souls never got the gospel of Jesus given to them for whatever reason. Although they may have the law implanted on their hearts from birth, these souls never got to see or feel it exercised in time/reality. Would it be wrong of God to give that soul another chance? How many chances have we been given in our life? Would you not want those multiple opportunities for your friends or family?

Some people may be getting upset over the idea that people (souls) get more than one opportunity to live life as if they know that the life they are living is their one and only opportunity in life. Now, if one got the opportunity to know about the love of our Lord and just flat-out denied the love of Christ, then so be it.

Another question I want to get you to consider: Is our Lord justified to do what He wants in showing mercy to the souls He possesses? This is the same Lord that told Peter, *"If I want him (the apostle John) to remain until I come, what is that to you? You follow Me!"* (John 21:21-22) So I will pose the question differently, what would it be to you if our Lord gave His souls second, third, or fourth opportunities to learn the knowledge of truth, and accept the love of Christ? It should be nothing to you because you just need to be worried about following Him.

THE GOD OF A SECOND CHANCE

For those who may be a little upset over the thought that God may give souls more than one opportunity at life, I am reminded of a few of Jesus's parables. One parable is about the landowner who hired laborers to work his vineyard (Matthew 20:1-16). At the end of the day, the landowner gave the same amount of pay to those who worked an entire day as those who worked only an hour. Those who worked longer were upset with the landowner and made their frustrations known. The landowner's response (verse 15) was this: *"Is it not lawful for me to do what I wish with what is my own? Or is your eye envious because I am generous?"* Wow! We are all God's. He can do what He wants with our souls and our lives.

Have you not been given favor, grace, and mercy? For many of us who were born in the United States, are we not better off than many of our fellow humans in other countries? We did nothing to deserve the country or family we were born into. We could've just as easily been born to a family or an area of the world that is not as fortunate to be free to learn of God's love.

For those who are still upset at the thought of souls getting more than one opportunity at life, consider the story of Jonah and the story of Jesus's encounter with the blind beggar Bartimaeus (Mark 10:46-52).

WERE THE PEOPLE OF NINEVEH WORTHY OF THEIR SOULS BEING SAVED?

In the book of Jonah, Jonah did not want to see the people of Nineveh saved because Nineveh was a wicked place. It was so perverse that its practices were well-known among other nations. The *great city* was full of wickedness and violence (Jonah 3:8). How full of wickedness was Nineveh? If I were to relate it to cities of today, it might be like Detroit and Las Vegas mixed. No disrespect to either city, but Detroit was rated as having one of the highest crime rates in numerous polls over the past few years, and Las Vegas is known as the "City of Sin."

Jonah felt that the people of Nineveh were undeserving of God's compassion and lovingkindness. Therefore, when he decided to run from his task of going to Nineveh and telling the people of the city to repent, he appointed himself as their judge. He had already condemned Nineveh and wanted them to remain in their sin, ultimately having God send them to their eternal death in hell.

God's answer to Jonah's disobedience and moral condemnation of Nineveh was this: *"Should I not have compassion on Nineveh, the great city in which there are more than 120,000 persons who do not know the difference between their right and left hand, as well as many animals?"* (Jonah 4:11 NASB). Here, we see that God was referring to those underdeveloped souls. He desires to see the innocent, the underdeveloped, and even the wicked saved. He wants the wicked to know Him, to turn from their ways, and to walk with Him.

RESTORING SIGHT

For many of us, it may seem that we do not want to see a lot of people given a chance at repentance like Jonah. Even worse, many of us do not think twice about those born into societies and environments different from our own—we often turn away from those who are less fortunate than ourselves. That is what the people in the story of the blind beggar Bartimaeus wanted Jesus to do—to turn away and keep walking.

Bartimaeus was one of those less fortunate souls; he was blind, a poor beggar, and down on his luck. If you believe in such matters as luck, then consider this: as Jesus was leaving the city of Jericho, Bartimaeus heard Him walking by.

Having heard of Christ and His miracles, Bartimaeus cried out, *"Jesus, Son of David, have mercy on me!"* He yelled out with all his soul. Although the disciples and other followers tried to quiet him, Bartimaeus cried out even louder, and Jesus called him over, ultimately restoring his sight.

There is much this passage can teach us about faith, biblical theology, and history—especially regarding the actions of the disciples and followers of Jesus. At that time, many Jewish people believed that a person's sin—or even their parent's sin—was the cause of their physical disabilities (John 9:1–3). In Bartimaeus's case, many thought his blindness was the result of his sin. So, when Christ's followers attempted to silence him, it was because they felt (or thought) they knew his sins and believed his sins were too great to allow Jesus to save him. Does God give chances like this to all of His children, no matter the situation?

UNDER THE MICROSCOPE: RAHAB AND THE CITY OF JERICHO

Returning to the Old Testament account of the Israelites' destruction of Jericho, Rahab's words to the spies (Joshua 2:8–12 NIV) reveal that many in the city recognized God's power. In this passage, Rahab declares, *"I know the Lord has given you this land and a great fear of you has fallen on us...our hearts melted in fear and everyone's courage failed because of you, for the Lord your God is God in heaven above and on the earth below."* Notice the emphasis in her words—a clear indication of her recognition of divine authority.

Hebrews 11:31(NIV) tells us that it was Rahab's faith that spared her and her family from being killed *"with those who were disobedient"* by the Israelites during their siege of Jericho. Now, wait a minute: it was not Rahab's faith in the spies but her genuine faith in God that saved her. This faith in God not only rescued her but eventually placed her in Christ's family tree (Matthew 1:5). Granted, Rahab was the one who took the spies in and hid them from the king's men—an act that gave her the opportunity to negotiate for her household's safety. Yet, her language—using words like *us, our,* and *everyone*—indicates that she was not alone in her belief. We can infer that many households in Jericho and throughout the Promised Land shared that conviction; it wasn't only Rahab's family that recognized that God was alive and powerful.

This example naturally leads us to consider a broader question: where was the opportunity for repentance for the other people of Jericho? Rahab's story suggests that while she was given a chance to express her faith both verbally and in action, others in her community were not afforded the same opportunity. No prophet was sent to Jericho to call them to repentance, as was done in Nineveh with Jonah. One might ask why these people were not given a chance—especially when the reputation of Nineveh was far worse than that of Jericho. Not even the children of Jericho were granted the opportunity to live a life reflective of God's mercy, as Rahab's family did.

Remember, God commanded the Israelites, via Moses and Joshua, to leave no man, woman, child, or animal alive. Are we to believe that our God—who does not desire for any of His children to see eternal death (Ezekiel 18:23, 32)—would send His people to kill those whose hearts had softened, simply because they believed that He was the God in heaven and on earth without a clear purpose? Are we to think that He only wanted to save one woman and her family so that she could become the ancestor of Jesus while allowing the rest of Jericho to perish? These are the very types of people that Christ came to save—those led astray but who have *seen the light* and whose hearts are softened and ready for repentance.

THE FATE OF UNDERDEVELOPED SOULS AND A NOTE ON ABORTION

This reflection on Rahab prompts a broader consideration: what is the fate of other souls, especially those that are underdeveloped or that never received a full opportunity for repentance? We do not know what happened to all the people of Jericho after they passed away. Still, we should consider that Rahab was not the only one who could have been given an opportunity for a full life—a life that enables one to learn, serve, glorify, and enjoy the God in heaven and on earth. While Rahab's documented faith provided her with that opportunity, what about the underdeveloped, led astray, or forgotten souls? Would God be just in giving them another chance at life?

Some have argued that all the children of Jericho would have gone to heaven after they were killed since they had no opportunity to knowingly sin. If that were the case, how then can we view the issue of abortion in the same way? If these underdeveloped souls in Jericho are automatically granted passage to heaven, then what distinguishes them from underdeveloped souls that are aborted?

If it is believed that the death of these souls did not serve a higher purpose, then something does not add up. Some argue that the people of Jericho were entirely disobedient and that their children would have grown up to be wicked as well—hence God's command to kill them (recall Ezekiel 18:20: *"The person who sins will die… the son will not bear the punishment for the father's iniquity, nor will the father bear the punishment for the son's iniquity"*). If that argument holds, then the debate on abortion must be reconsidered. If a child, once born into a disobedient home, exacerbates societal wickedness, then preventing its birth might seem justified by that reasoning.

So, while some view every fetus as a living soul deserving a chance to develop, others point out that certain circumstances of conception lead to environments that are detrimental. God wants Christians to act righteously, govern themselves, and let their example of Godly living be the light and example to the world (Matthew 5:14-16). God tells Moses that if the nation of Israel is obedient, that they will be blessed and they will have the fear and respect of other nations. They will be the *head* of society and not *the tail* (Deuteronomy 28:1-14). Christians are trying to avoid more disobedient people in society; thus, abortion could be viewed as an acceptable option to diminish disobedience and wickedness.

For some, the question of abortion is simple: if the child inside a woman is a living soul, is it moral to end the life of an innocent soul? Those who view it this way believe that every soul should be given a chance to navigate its environment. Pro-life supporters note that people come from various households—Christian or non-Christian—and that both can produce souls that either develop in a godly direction or not. Therefore, every child, every underdeveloped soul, deserves the opportunity to fully develop its ultimate resting place, and no decision by a human should prematurely cut that process short. For others, abortion involves weighing the circumstances of conception and the potential hardships—poverty, crime, discrimination, abuse—that the child may face once born. Pro-choice supporters raise these issues separately, questioning who will care for the child if the parents are unable, and whether those advocating pro-life are willing to fund and accept responsibility for the child's upbringing. Pro-choice supporters believe that if one says they are Pro-life, they must be about the entire life of that individual, not just the birth. They must support those children's health and education, their growth as well as the health and welfare of their parents, not just the events surrounding them coming into this world.

Ultimately, the legal system—which has removed God from its basis—cannot resolve the spiritual question of abortion, for every individual has the right to define who they are and what they do with their body, provided it does not infringe on the rights of others. Everyone's situation is different. Some children are conceived under circumstances that God never intended for His people to experience, and it remains our responsibility as Christians to follow Christ and love our neighbor.

A NOTE ON COMPASSION, REPENTANCE, AND ADDITIONAL CHANCES

Many of us feel as if we know better than our Lord, like Jonah, and we want to keep people—whom we deem to have sins worse than our own—away from Christ's love. But in doing so, we deny them growth; we keep them from experiencing a relationship—a walk—with the Lord.

Consider Mark 10:52: What did Bartimaeus do after he was restored and saved? He began following Jesus, discarding his old life and cloak and embarking on an entirely new path. Think about how many people never get the chance to be called or answer the call from the Lord because we assume we are protecting heaven. Could God not do what He can and have compassion for the underdeveloped and shut-out souls?

We assume, like Jonah and Christ's followers, that

everyone has had their chance to receive the call. But what if you were or are their Jonah? How many children or less fortunate—or even wealthy—souls have you ignored, hated, or justified turning away from? Would God be wrong in giving that soul another chance at a different life or call? The answer is no.

CONCLUDING THOUGHTS ON GOD'S SOVEREIGNTY AND ENDLESS LOVE

In the end, these reflections underscore a profound truth: offering additional chances for underdeveloped souls does not alter God's nature or His moral code—it only magnifies His love, mercy, and commitment to ensuring every soul has the opportunity to know, glorify, and enjoy Him. Whether a child's earthly life is brief or an adult never encounters Christ's love, God's unsearchable mercy may grant further opportunities.

Ultimately, the way we live on earth—exercising our power to define, choose, and follow God—forms the foundation for our eternal destiny. As we embrace His endless love and live out His commandments, we are drawn ever closer to His light, trusting that His sovereign design will bring every soul into His eternal embrace.

GIVING U.P.
Thoughts

Conversation Seven
ON EARTH AS IT IS IN HEAVEN
Can we relate earthly love to heavenly order?

Do you believe that the way one lives on Earth will be exactly the way one lives in Heaven, or is there an expectation of a transformed existence? Reflect on the words, *"On earth as it is in heaven..."* which Christ taught His disciples in prayer. These words invite constant contemplation and serve as a reminder that earthly conduct is closely linked to the eternal order that awaits. Faithful believers prepare for their heavenly destiny even as they live on Earth.

One thing we fail to do here on Earth is think about Heaven and its systems or processes. We don't relate how we govern here to how Heaven is governed. We don't think the community God has in Heaven may differ significantly from what we set up here. We fail to relate the love we share on Earth to how it is shared in Heaven.

God is the Creator of the poor, the middle class, the rich, of all races and every creature; yet some still act as if superiority is determined by uncontrollable attributes. The problem with us so-called Christians is we make our God look like something He never showed or told us. We are not forgiving. We try to block rights or privileges away from others by misusing the name of the LORD or using some twisted interpretation of His commandments. Sometimes, we do this out of love, and sometimes, we do this out of hate. In either event, no one was ever instructed to force God upon others.

GOD'S REPRESENTATIVES

Consider this: believers are meant to be a light. A light does not impose itself where it is unwelcome; it simply shines. God intended the Israelites to inherit the Promised Land and to walk in His statutes so that their lives would serve as an example for others, not as a means to force His laws upon surrounding nations or to return to Egypt and impose His ways. The joy and peace experienced under the rule of the LORD were meant to be so compelling that others would declare, *"I want that,"* and inquire about the true God being worshiped.

Imposing personal agendas or distorted interpretations of divine commandments does not reflect the Lord's intention. Do not distort the intentions of our LORD. Do not distort His image. Do not misrepresent His kingdom in Heaven. If you do this, you are not a reflection of His light. You are not a disciple or His kingdom's ambassador. You are your own king and ambassador of your own agenda and standard. Your standard is no better than the people you are trying to get to follow you. The only high standard is the LORD's. Revelation 7:9-10 (NASB) states:

> *After these things I looked, and behold, a great multitude which no one could count, from every nation and all the tribes, peoples, and languages, standing before the throne and before the Lamb, clothed in white robes, and palm branches were in their hands; and they cried out with a loud voice, saying, 'Salvation belongs to our God who sits on the throne, and to the Lamb.'*

If people from every nation, tribe, and language, clothed alike, are united in praise in Heaven, then why is there segregation among believers on Earth? Earth is the training ground for the eternal home, and perspectives should be refined here rather than waiting for an automatic change in Heaven. Why do we think that God will automatically change our perspective of others once we reach Heaven, especially since we had the opportunity and requirement to do it here on Earth?

The entire law is fulfilled by loving one's neighbor as oneself (Galatians 5:14). Therefore, if love for neighbors is neglected, discrimination prevails, or others are hindered in any way, it contradicts the law given by Christ. Galatians 5:15 (CSB) states, *"But if you bite and devour one another, watch out, or you will be consumed by one another."* Not only are we destroying ourselves and whatever beautiful opportunity God would want to bless us with here on Earth, but we are also destroying whatever glorious blessings Christ wants to prepare for us in Heaven. With our own actions, we consume not only our earthly blessings but also our heavenly blessings.

Many become blinded by earthly possessions, status,

and personal legacies, failing to see the ruin inflicted on themselves and on others—a condition reminiscent of the scribes, Pharisees, and hypocrites described in Matthew 23, for whom Christ expressed deep lament. We are the scribes and Pharisees, the hypocrites, blind guides, and snakes that are condemning ourselves. If how it is on Earth is how it is in Heaven, there is no wonder why Christians and our God get a bad rap. We make ourselves look despicable and our Lord absurd and foolish. If how it is on Earth is how it is in Heaven, who would want to spend an eternity there?

A closing thought on the matter of earthly living and eternal order: The words of Christ, *"On earth as it is in heaven,"* call for a present reflection of unity, forgiveness, and oneness. When hate and fear are held onto, every moment diminishes love and peace and prevents the fulfillment of divine purpose. If every second of hate causes the loss of what once inspired love, then it is imperative to choose compassion over conflict. Aligning earthly behavior with heavenly values ensures that the legacy of love and unity is not only preserved but becomes a testimony to the eternal nature of God's kingdom. Ultimately, the way life is lived on Earth serves as both a mirror and a preparation for the order and love that will define the eternal home.

Holding on to Hate, Letting Go of God

Each second we hold on to hate & fear,
we let go of love.
Each second we hold on to hate & fear,
we let go of peace.
Each second we hold on to hate & fear,
we stop being what our loved ones fell in love with.
Each second we hold on to hate & fear,
we stop fulfilling our purpose.
Each second we hold on to hate & fear,
we turn our backs to God to embrace the evil one.
At all costs, hold on to love.

GIVING U.P.
Thoughts

Conversation Eight
MANKIND'S CONTINUED DOCUMENTATION
Is continuing the written legacy of God really that important?

In school, was history one of your favorite subjects? Some people do not enjoy learning history. Some might say, *"It already happened, so why should I care?"* Knowing one's history is essential. If you do not know where you came from, how will you know what things to avoid or actions to repeat?

Carter G. Woodson, the creator of Black History Week, the precursor to Black History Month, believed, *"If a race has no history, it has no worthwhile tradition, it becomes a negligible factor in the thought of the world, and it stands in danger of being exterminated."*[5] The history of a race, a family, or anything must be continually documented and presented in such a way as to be made relatable to current cultures and its issues for the traditions to remain desirable and the race, family, or thing to remain a significant factor in the thought of whatever environment they operate. I must be clear:

---
5 (Woodson, C. G. (April 1926). "Negro History Week." Journal of Negro History.)

history must not be changed or falsified to make it seem more desirable or acceptable. Truth and facts must not be skewed to favor any agenda. History must be authentically documented and taught.

Our failure to routinely document the Lord's current impact on our lives and make it relatable puts our faith in danger of being exterminated or, worse, rewritten. I believe our faith being rewritten is worse because having no sense of God is not as detrimental as having a corrupted and disgraceful image of God. A new faith can be discovered, a lost faith can be found and rejuvenated, but a rewritten faith is corrupted, and the original faith and intent are at risk of being lost forever.

In the media and on social networks, a great movement is aimed at rewriting, reimaging, rebranding, and canceling who our God is and how He loves us. This act needs to be combatted with the truth of the love of our Lord. We need to make honoring God's glory, His true glory, a priority in our lives as believers and disciples of Christ.

What I am about to say next may seem counter to the point I want to make, but be patient and continue reading. I will show you how our love and idolized outlook of the past can taint our current and future relationship with God.

GOD OF THEN AND NOW

Our love for the classical and our need to separate the glorious history from the seemingly flawed present has perverted mankind's view of the living God. Americans are enamored with the past. We have television shows such as

Antiques Roadshow and Wonder Years. We love movies on the Ten Commandments, the Wild West, the Civil War, and the War for American Independence. We love movies about King Arthur or the Empire of Rome. We have slogans like "Make America Great Again" and "Remember the good ol' days." We love to perceive the past as a time in our history that was more glorious and something that we lost. Humanity is taught to believe this and hold a perspective like this because current believers misunderstand how we are supposed to see our God.

The issue with us Christians is that we look at the Bible and even our God the same way. We see our Father as the Lord of the Bible, the Deity of the Early A.D., and not the Holy Here and Now. We think His work on Earth and in the lives of humankind is over. As a result of this thinking, we left our first love in the past. We lost our infatuation for our Savior. This belief has caused many of us to distort our faith and relationship with Him because we don't think He is still concerned with His church and us as individuals, as He did in the Bible. However, this is not true.

He is still alive and working to this day. The Lord still loves and bestows blessings. The Spirit, the Helper, still moves and breathes life into creation. We, as believers, should document this: His current work. Our failure to document and socialize the Lord's work in our lives has left many with a sense that God is not an accessible source of love, guidance, and help. One reason for this is our failure to talk about the Lord, which has made it difficult for us to understand who God is and how involved He is in our lives. Therefore, we can't see His work, which is taking place right in front of us.

ACKNOWLEDGE GOD

Why is this continued documentation and glorification of our Lord essential for us today? For starters, our Lord God is a jealous God. He wants our time and attention. He wants to be glorified and honored. He wants His name to be praised and honored in our mouths. He wants His agenda, His *legacy* pushed, not ours. He wants people who are after His heart to do His will. We can't do any of these things our Lord desires by primarily focusing on our own selfish desires, prestige, or legacy. We do that far too often, desiring to tell our own story or build monuments to our greatness for ourselves. Whether that greatness is personal, group, program, or country, it still shifts attention away from the Lord's will and intent for us.

When this happens, it angers our Heavenly Father. Once our Father is upset with our way of life or feeling forgotten, He introduces changes into our lives that show us (as believers and unbelievers alike) that we need to shift our focus back to Him. One of the best examples of God introducing changes into His people's lives is the story of the Tower of Babel (Genesis 11:1-9). We see a group of people chasing after their own legacy and self-gratification instead of their Lord's legacy.

In the story of the Tower of Babel, we learn that everyone speaks the same language. A large group or clan decided to come together to build a city, a tall tower. Two reasons are noted (verse 4) for their desire to build the city and the tower.

The first reason was to make a name for themselves. Second, the people wanted to stop spreading out. They wanted to remain in one place and stop scattering abroad over the Earth. To sum up the people's two reasons, the people of Babel wanted to make themselves the focus of humanity and, for lack of better terms, the center of the universe.

God recognized their desires and the potential humans had to achieve those desires. The Lord said in verse six, *"Nothing which they plan to do will be impossible (inaccessible) for them."* (NASB 2020) So, the Lord introduced two changes into their lives to interrupt their two goals. He confused their language and spread the group of people around the Earth. The Lord geographically repositioned that group of people around the Earth, so there was no way they could try to remain in one place.

But what does this have to do with God's glory? Did you notice that the people did not acknowledge God before or during the building process? Humankind reached great heights without the slightest thought of including God or honoring Him and His glory. It was not the fact that they were unified that angered God. It was not the fact that they were becoming technologically advanced. The issue arose when there was no thought or mention of the God that blessed them to achieve such heights. The people had everything they needed to build and the environment to sustain their living in that area, but they gave no thanks for these resources, which the Creator gave.

The greatest gift God gave humanity, other than Christ, is time (opportunity). The greatest tool that God gave humanity to navigate through time is communication and reason (verbal and nonverbal). What did this group do with their opportunity, communication, and reason? They did not use these resources to give thanks to the Provider. So, God introduced changes.

God wants you to enjoy the life He has given you, but be sure to acknowledge and be thankful for the life you have received. Solomon wrote in Ecclesiastes, *"Don't let the excitement of youth cause you to forget the Creator."* In other words, do not let your desires for life, work, or even family seduce or distract you from honoring the One that gave you what you have. Solomon also states, enjoy the fruits of your labor, in Ecclesiastes, but concludes that one must fear, respect, and obey God. We can quickly lose what we have received and worked so hard for if we neglect to acknowledge and thank our Lord.

Another reason this continued documentation and glorification of our Lord is important is that it provides new believers (young and old) with more relatable stories of the goodness of our Lord. These accounts of God must be easily consumable and applicable to their lives. Writing down our stories gives future generations something more current and tangible that can be traced. These new believers or those questioning where to place their faith can see and speak with the people whose lives God has significantly impacted.

A major reason so many young men and women are not looking to God more often or at all is because they don't have current examples of God working in people's lives. I am talking about everyday examples. I am not talking about the magnificent examples of God at work. Although more stories of those are needed, many people don't know how much God has influenced their lives or the lives of those around them.

DISOBEDIENT OR DISTRACTED?

Look at the world today. With the advent of social media and increased dependency on social media, humans are flooded with images and stories about everything. We are seduced and distracted by news and short videos of things we don't need but are influenced into thinking we do. We have this unconscious desire to be updated with issues or stories that don't affect our lives or require our attention. And we don't know that these things are taking us away from where the Lord wants us and where our focus should be.

Our ability to access whatever we want with the push of a button or swipe of a finger has made many of us think that we need to know everything happening on this globe. Many humans have not realized that much of the information is chaff to them. In the military, chaff are things that seduce or distract us away from the intended target or objective. It confuses us and is nothing more than a worthless obstruction to which we do not need to dedicate any of our time or mind. When we dedicate our time to those things, we unknowingly are drawn away from seeing what God is doing in our lives or God's objectives for us.

Let's go back to the story of the Tower of Babel. Those people were drawn away from thinking about God and fulfilling one of God's directives given to Noah and his family after the Flood. What was that objective? Read Genesis 9 Verse 1. One of the first things God told Noah after he and his family left the ark was to multiply and fill the Earth. What did the people building the tower not want to do? They did not want to fill or be scattered across the Earth (Genesis 11:4).

I do not believe they were intentionally trying to disobey God. They did not know, at this time, since time had elapsed between God speaking to Noah and the building of the tower. God's command to Noah and his descendants may not have been passed down as a requirement for humanity, so the people did what sounded right and logical in their own eyes. Therefore, continuing to document what God has commanded us to do and what God has done in our lives is important. Doing so keeps us on the righteous path God wants us to be on and gives future generations the message that God is still alive and cares about what we do. If the group building the tower had received that word, then God may not have changed our ability to easily communicate with each other. Our unintentional mistakes can result in unintended consequences.

WHAT HAPPENS WHEN YOU INCLUDE GOD

Some may ask what God has done that is so special that we believers can talk about it to new believers and those questioning where to place their faith. Like I said earlier, it doesn't have to be something miraculous. The Bible gives plenty of examples of situations where God gave something some may call small but made an enormous impact.

MANKIND'S CONTINUED DOCUMENTATION

The story of Samuel is one of answered prayers. It is a story that if only hearing about the answered prayer of Samuel's mother, and not how that prayer impacted an entire nation, one would not fully see how God is at work in our lives and how He uses our prayers to fulfill His will and positively impact the lives of many.

Samuel's mother, Hannah, was childless. Desperately wanting a child, she took her desire to the Lord in prayer. She promised the Lord that if He answered her prayer, she would give the child back to the Lord, and her son would be His for his entire lifetime (I Samuel 1:11). The following year, she received her child, Samuel. As promised, after weaning young Samuel, Hannah took her son back to the Tabernacle to be a priest and servant of the house of the Lord.

If stopping there in the story, one might see Hannah's situation as an isolated incident that could be explained as Hannah and her husband not coming together at the right time of the month or something insignificant and common. It is simply a minor fulfillment of one woman's desire not to be publicly humiliated because she could not bear children. At that time, a woman who could not have children was considered a disgrace to some, cursed by God since they were not able to be fruitful and do their part in continuing the family line. But as you read on and finish the books of Samuel, one sees that Hannah's prayer impacted not only herself but the entire nation of Israel, including the lives of the first two kings of Israel, Saul and David.

Why is this important? What can we learn from this?

THE IMPACT OF PRAYER

First, God hears the prayers of those who call out to Him and earnestly seek Him, no matter how seemingly insignificant, unimportant, or unknown one may be to society or the bigger picture of a nation. God loves all His children, those who love Him. (Jeremiah 29:12-13, 1 Peter 3:12, 1 John 5:14)

Second, God knows our hearts. If Hannah wanted a child for selfish reasons that would not benefit, glorify, or honor our Lord, I don't think God would have fulfilled her prayer. We know that her heart was in the right place by her vow to the Lord. Although she did not want to be humiliated by her peers or seen as anything less than a blessed woman to her husband, she still made a vow to God that if He gave her the child, she would give it back to serve Him. Even though she wanted Samuel and loved her son, she still gave him back to the Lord. God's will and legacy were still intertwined with her desire.

Lastly, this is important: God uses our seemingly insignificant prayers to impact the national or international picture. He works His will through us by our glorification of and communication with Him. Understand that prayer is our greatest tool or means to change our lives.

Our glorification of Him is a testimony that can bring others closer to God. He likes to use the small, disabled, and seemingly insignificant things or people to do big and impactful things. This act is seen in the stories of the Bible, such as Gideon versus Midianites, David versus Goliath,

Daniel in captivity, and Jesus and the Samaritan woman. Documenting these events connects all the pieces to the puzzle to see the greater picture. The Bible is a series of separate documented events, and the greater picture and message of the Bible would not be known if someone had not documented these stories or thoughts.

Our lack of documentation and glorification of our God today has many people and future generations missing valuable pieces of the greater picture, which is God's will and intent for His people and this Earth. It also paints a picture that God's work and care for this Earth and its inhabitants ceased after the writings of the Bible were consolidated and put together. That couldn't be further from the truth.

MY FAMILY TREE

Take my family's story. My being here and writing this work are the direct results of God's grace and influence on my family's lives. My parents are from Mobile, Alabama. They went to rival high schools. My mother went to Blount High School. My father went to Williamson High School. My dad played football. My mother was the football team's sweetheart. They had mutual friends growing up but never met each other until college. They met at a small college, Bishop College, in Dallas, Texas.

My father is the fourth of nine children. He grew up in a single-parent home after his father died when my father was in elementary school. He would say they grew up poorer than poor. Every child had a responsibility or chore(s) inside the home. Once you were old enough, that responsibility transferred outside the home in the form of a paying job.

Overcoming attention and focus issues while in middle school, my father worked to earn a selection to the National Honor Society during his ninth-grade year. Prior to earning that achievement, the faculty at his school placed my father in *special classes* because the faculty thought he had a learning disability. My father's issue was not a learning disability. Rather, he just had a battle with maintaining his focus during class. Maybe his focus issues stemmed from lacking a father figure in the home. My father's father died while my father was a young child. My father did not know the cause of his focus issues in school, but he recognized where the faculty placed him was not where he wanted to be and used it as motivation to get his academic career in order. He maintained high academic standards throughout high school, graduate, and postgraduate education, eventually earning his MBA from Dallas Baptist University.

My mother grew up in a six-member home, her parents, her two brothers, her sister, and herself. She grew up wanting what her parents had, a six-member home, two-parent household, with two boys and two girls. She also wanted twins. Another amazing thing about the story is my mother heard fantastic stories about the city of Dallas as a young girl and desired to go there as an adult. Also, before she ever met my father, she wanted to marry an accountant, enamored by their nice suits and stable lifestyle.

There is so much to this story, but I will give you the abridged version for the sake of time. My mom and dad would end up in class together in Dallas, Texas, from Mobile, Alabama. They met shortly after my dad changed his major from History to Accounting. They would later get married and have two boys and two twin girls. My mother got her two-parent, six-person household, with two boys and two (twin) girls. Again, there is so much more to this story that makes it so much greater of a story than what I am telling you now, but if one took each independent incident and only looked at that, they would not get the bigger picture of how the Lord is working on something greater, not just in our lives, but of those around us.

Now, if one were to take my parents' story and couple it with my story and how a kid from Dallas, TX, never once considered a career in the Navy, became a graduate of the United States Naval Academy and a 20+ year career Naval Officer. Then, part of my story includes my parents meeting a young Tony Evans, a world-renowned pastor in Dallas. Fast forward to Dr. Tony Evans' son Jonathan getting me into football in the spring of my junior year of high school. Unbeknownst to Jonathan, he helped pave the way for my answered prayer. In high school, I prayed that my parents did not have to pay for me to attend college. That prayer was answered in the form of an appointment to the United States Naval Academy via recruitment in football. All these seemingly insignificant things could easily be overlooked or seen as luck, but to someone who sees the bigger picture, they know it is God at work.

OUR STORY, OUR TESTIMONY

So many people have a story like my family's. So many believers have testimonies of small, seemingly insignificant incidents that add up to a big, beautiful story of the Lord's hand at work in their lives. These are the types of stories that God wants you to share. It does not have to be a story of some kid moving a car or someone saving the lives of tens or hundreds. It is the daily things that the Lord wants us to share. Why? Because these are the events that show that the Lord is with us daily. These stories show that God still walks with those who want to walk with Him. These stories keep our traditions worthwhile, continue God's legacy, and stop us from being a negligible factor in the thought of the world.

Do not lose sight of what the Bible shows us about documenting the Lord's work in our day-to-day lives. If you are not already, start documenting how the Lord walks with you and impacts your life. If not for you, write, record, or film it for your children and the next generation of disciples who need your testimony, inspiration, and direction. You may not know it, but the fruits of your documentation will continue to grow for years, decades, and centuries to come.

THE BUILDING IS NOT THE GOAL

Do not lose sight of this either. Christ came to establish His family, which would grow into a great community and nation. His goal is not to build an institution or business for the sole sake of Christian's economic advancement.

For many churches, the church has become their business institution for economic gain or personal popularity, not their discipleship business. Many churches desire to gain more members, not believers and disciples for Christ. They seek more members and people in the pews for popularity and profit. Their focus is not on the love of God spreading and the glorification of His name becoming commonplace.

The church today has become some Christian leaders' Tower of Babel. Our focus shifted to creating something tall, a great institution for the sake of ourselves. We desire that our church has a great eternal name so more people will come to it for years to come. All along, we forgot about the great name of our Heavenly Father. Scratch that--we did not forget about it. We pushed His name aside because we forgot how great and powerful His name is.

We must glorify El Elyon's name throughout the years to come and for future generations, not a name we made for ourselves or our church. Although our name may come from the Bible, or our church name may reference our Lord, although we may give a shout-out to our savior at church events, we forgot, or we were never taught how to really glorify God with our entire being.

So, how do you do this? Say thank you to the Lord and tell others about His goodness in your life and the lives of others around you. Honor or magnify His name more than you do your own or your church's name. Be more eager and excited to talk about His greatness as you are to talk about your favorite sports teams' or businesses' wins. Be grateful for the Lord's love, mercy, and grace that He showers upon you daily.

GIVING U.P.
Thoughts

Conversation Nine
JOHN THE BAPTIST
Was John the Baptist doubtful or doubtless?

What is your relationship with doubt? In the quiet moments of reflection, doubt likes to creep in, whispering questions that linger long after the voices of assurance have faded. Doubt doesn't always have to last, though. Sometimes, it's a flicker that fades away seconds after it sparks. Everyone has had doubts in their lives, big or small--doubt even befriended some of the heroes we've read about in the Bible. John the Baptist was said to have doubted Jesus as the Messiah.

Though, I propose that John never doubted who Christ was. Even when facing death in prison, John's faith in Christ never waned. John's sending of his disciples to Jesus while he was imprisoned was for their benefit, not John's own reassurance. John did not want his faithful disciples to lose faith in Christ. He knew that his disciples needed to hear the motivating words of Christ, *"The blind see, the lame walk, the lepers are cleansed, the deaf hear, the dead are raised, the poor have the gospel preached to them. And blessed is he who is not offended because of Me"* (Luke 7:22-23).

How is John's faith and understanding of his role in God's kingdom important for us today? We will see that we can learn some unexpected lessons from John the Baptist.

INTERTWINED WITH THE SPIRIT

When looking at John the Baptist's life, it is apparent that John understood his role within the will of God and his importance to the ministry of Christ. John knew that he had to decrease in his disciples' eyes so Christ could increase in their eyes. John did this already when he allowed two of his disciples to leave him and follow Jesus (John 1:19-42). John knew before Christ started his ministry that Jesus was the Messiah, and he told people so.

Even before John was born, he felt in his spirit the awesomeness and presence of Christ. Luke Chapter 1, Verses 39-45, describes a meeting between John's mother, Elizabeth, and Jesus's mother, Mary, when Elizabeth was six months pregnant with John. When John heard the voice of Jesus's mother, Mary, he *leaped for joy* inside his mother's womb. Before he took his first breath outside the womb, John the Baptist had a sense of who Mary was and who Christ would be to the world. John's spirit became overjoyed because of the hope, truth, and love his cousin, Jesus, was about to bring to the lost and misguided souls of the world.

One could even argue, even if John did not have a sense of who Mary or Jesus was, the spirit that rested upon him or that moved within him knew who Mary and Jesus would be to the world, and that spirit expressed its joy through baby John the Baptist in his mother's womb. We have all seen or experienced it. How often have we been in church and the preacher said something that sent a tingle through our body or listened to a song and could not control the tears coming down our cheeks or the warm sensation moving through our body?

In Romans 8:26-27, the Bible talks about the Spirit interceding for us and expressing things to God on our behalf. This action could be what happened to John the Baptist inside Elizabeth's womb. That leap of joy John displayed could have been the spirit showing reverence to Jesus and respect to the woman who would carry the future Messiah. In either case, whatever was deep within John that wanted to worship Christ was there before birth.

JOHN'S BELIEF

This strong faith in Christ and understanding of who He was continued for John after he started his ministry in the wilderness before Jesus ever started His ministry. In the books of Matthew, Mark, and John (Matthew 3:11-14; Mark 1:7-8; John 1:29-42, 3:25-36), the reader sees John the Baptist's recognition of who Jesus was. Not only do we see his recognition of who Jesus was, but we also see John's understanding of his role in preparing a way for Jesus's ministry.

In Matthew 3 and Mark 1, John states that he is not worthy of even holding Jesus's sandals. At the time, slaves or servants, when their master would come home, would take the sandals from their feet to clean their feet and sandals. John held Jesus in such high esteem that he felt he was not worthy enough to be called a slave of Christ. Think about that. Think about how much respect and honor you must have for someone to think that about yourself. John also stated that the baptism he was conducting was nothing like the baptism Jesus would conduct. His description of his own work and Christ's work shows that he felt their missions, although connected, could not be compared. John's words clearly show he knew who Christ was.

We also see John understanding the importance of his overt testimony that Jesus is the Messiah, and he was just a messenger who came to prepare a path for Christ. In John 1: 29-34, John plainly states that someone sent him for the ministry of baptism and to prepare a path for the one who comes after him. Also, he states that Jesus is the *Chosen One.* The next day, after making these statements, John encourages two of his disciples to follow Jesus by telling them that Jesus is the Lamb of God (John 1:35-39). This passage shows that John confidently knew who Jesus was, so much so that he encouraged his followers to leave him and follow Christ.

John's confidence in Christ and understanding of his place within Christ's ministry is further displayed in John 3:25-36. John states in verse 30, *"He (Jesus) must increase, but I must decrease."* John was preparing his disciples. His followers were devoted to him to the point that they were jealous of Jesus and his disciples getting more followers than John. John let them know in this passage that this was supposed to happen. People are supposed to follow Jesus, not him (John). He tells them in verse 36, *"He that believes in the Son has eternal life..."* John had the complete picture. John knew that Christ came to set people's eyes on eternal life and the eternal kingdom of God in heaven.

John knew that Christ did not come to reign on Earth at that time. We know this because John's ministry was about repentance and getting your heart right with the LORD. If his ministry were meant to prepare man for an earthly kingdom reign of Christ, John would have prepared the people for war, law, and order, not for the forgiveness of sins.

I contend that John never doubted who Christ was. He knew before birth who Christ was and would be and maintained that belief through death. His words and actions throughout his ministry show that John the Baptist truly believed that Christ was the Messiah and Chosen One who was above all and would give eternal life to those who would follow and believe in Him.

FINDING YOUR PLACE

So, how does this help us today? We learn two important lessons from John's faith in Christ and his understanding of his position within God's kingdom ministry. First, we learn the importance of knowing and understanding our role within God's kingdom and how that helps us maintain our faith. Realizing that it is not all about us keeps us focused on God's plan and purpose for us. Second, we learn it's not about our pastor, priest, bishop, or church leader. Following them, or even the person who introduced you to Christ, won't get you into Heaven. Gaining an understanding and perspective that it is your own personal relationship for you to build with Christ is your key to the kingdom.

John knew his role within the kingdom and knew his place was not to outshine or try to be equal to Jesus. John the Baptist knew that it was Christ who was supposed to be great in the people's eyes. He tells his disciples that his purpose is to prepare the path for Christ. So, John knew his assigned task. Again, John told his disciples that he must decrease in their eyes, and Jesus must increase in their eyes. Understanding these two things helped John maintain confidence in Christ. Even when imprisoned and facing death, John remained steadfast because he knew that it was not about him. He knew there was something greater, beyond the fame or power the world could give, that God had in store for him.

Our initial focus should be to find our purpose within God's ministry. Second, understand that our purpose is not to promote ourselves but Christ. Whatever task God assigned us down here, we know it is not about our earthly glory but Christ's earthly glory. We may become well known because of our kingdom's work here on Earth. Man may put us on a pedestal, like they did John, but understand, like John, that the purpose is to prepare and lead people to Christ, not acquire new followers.

FOLLOWER COUNT

Speaking of following, who are you following? I see many people take pride in attending a popular pastor's church.

Many people take pride in following a specific person in the ministry on social media sites. I've even seen some people feel that they are *good* with God because their mother, father, or grandparent is a spiritual person. Some people think that following these well-known people or having a Christian in the family is their birthright into the kingdom of Heaven.

John shows us that it is not about following people or even being related to them. It is about following Christ and having a relationship with Him. John was popular during his ministry. Priests, Levites, Pharisees, and Sadducees came out to see him. People from around Judea came out to be baptized by him. He had disciples before Christ did.

It's what John told his disciples that is of great importance. When he told his disciples that Jesus must become greater in their eyes and he must become less in their eyes, John was telling them that following him wouldn't get them where they needed to go. While in prison, when he sent his disciples to see Jesus, that was his hand-off to the Messiah. They needed to see Jesus, hear his voice, and listen to his words to fully understand who and what John was saying throughout his entire ministry.

John's disciples needed to know that building their own relationship with Christ and not just listening to and following John was the most important thing they would do. John the Baptist was the appetizer to the main course in Christ. The leader of your church or the person you follow on social media may be your appetizer, but you are missing what will fill you up. If you continue to follow them and do not develop your own relationship with your Lord, you are not getting fully fed.

The intent is for you to walk your own walk with your Lord. Seek your own understanding. As you walk with the Lord and gain more wisdom and understanding, you will be given a new perspective on the Bible and the world around you. With this new perspective, you will become as confident as John in your role in God's kingdom.

Conversation Ten
REMAIN IN YOUR BAPTISM

How do you make sure you don't leave the spirit at the water?

What does it mean to be truly transformed? For many, the answer is the sacred act of baptism—a powerful symbol of rebirth and commitment. Most believers have been baptized at least once in their lives. Depending on the church, the baptism occurred inside a pool or outside in a still body of water. Either way, once dipped, you came up with the feeling that you were a new person. With that act, it is over, and you can move on. Right?

I attended and sometimes led a Bible study at Father Joe's Village, a homeless shelter in San Diego, California. As I think about John the Baptist's ministry and the importance of him *fulfilling all righteousness* through baptizing Christ, I am reminded of a lesson I learned during one of the Bible studies at Father Joe's Village. One evening, Chaplain Michael Hakanson said something that opened my eyes as I had never heard someone refer to one's baptism in such a way. I am paraphrasing his words. He said, *"We don't look at our baptism as something that we are under or in. We don't see it as something that we continuously live with or within. We look at our baptism as a single act or event in our lives. We see it as something that took place on a certain date that many of us forget."*

That is how I looked at it. It was a check in the box for me. I was baptized in my preteen years. Although I understood my decision and what it meant to get baptized, I did not fully understand the significance of my decision and the follow-on responsibilities that came with the public declaration of my faith. That complete understanding came later. For many, the knowledge that our baptism is something that we work to remain under is something that is lost or never explained to us.

REMAIN IN BAPTISM

In Mark 10:38 (NASB), Jesus asks James and John, *"Are you able to be baptized with the baptism with which I am baptized?"* Jesus refers to "the baptism" as something He is presently in. He uses the words *I am*, not *I was*. So, what was Jesus baptized with? What remained on Him throughout His ministry and life? It was the Holy Spirit (John 1:32).

Someone might be thinking, *well, that was back then, and that was Jesus. What about now? What about me right now? How does this apply to me today? How do I know the Spirit is with me now?*

JOHN 14:15-26

In this passage, Jesus tells his disciples, *"If you love Me, you will keep my commandments. I will ask the Father, and He will give you another Helper, that He may be with you forever; that is the Spirit of truth... He abides with you and will be in you (v. 15-18)."* Pay special attention to verse 18. *"I [Jesus] will not leave you as orphans; I will come to you."*

When you accept Jesus as Savior and do so with a public proclamation (baptism), you are not only saying you want to go to Heaven to spend eternity with the Lord, whom you trust and believe in, you are saying you are immersing yourself into a new lifestyle here on earth. The word *baptism/baptize* means to immerse. When baptized, one is not just immersing themselves in water. They are immersing themselves in a new life and into a new family.

Again, pay special attention to verse 18. Focus on the word *orphans*. When we choose to put our faith in Jesus Christ as our Savior and Director, we are not left as orphans with no representation or direction. Rather, we are adopted into the family of the Most High God with God as our Father (Galatians 4:4-6 and Ephesians 1:5).

With this adoption comes responsibilities. I would tell my sailors who worked for me that whenever your boss changes, your job description changes. Each person has their own way of running their division, department, or branch. Similarly, whenever you enter someone's house, you fall under their rules whether you are a part of their family or not. When God adopts you, you are expected to abide by the

Lord's rules and commands.

KEEPING HIS COMMANDS

Go back to John 14:15-26. Jesus says multiple times to keep His commands. He wanted His disciples to understand the importance of keeping His commands, so he restated it. Whether you realize it or not, you have a part in keeping the Holy Spirit with you. Each of us is responsible for keeping the Holy Spirit within us nurtured, strengthened, and happy.

Remember, Jesus said in verse 16 that the Holy Spirit *may* be with you forever. *May* is the important word. He did not say the Holy Spirit *will* or *has to* be with you forever. This means the Spirit can intercede in your life or let your rule reign in your life. If you do not empower the Spirit inside you with the word of the Lord, then the Spirit won't feel empowered to intervene in your thinking and affairs. The Spirit will not always speak to you to push you into the right decision or direction. The Spirit gauges whether you want its input or not, and it gauges how often you nurture it with the word from the Bible. The freedom of choice still resides with you as a human and believer in Christ.

So, what choice do we have the freedom to make? We have daily decisions, such as obeying the commands of the Lord or choosing a different direction. These may come in the form of minor decisions, seemingly insignificant matters, or major decisions that may have ramifications that affect not only our lives but the lives of others.

Some of you may still be thinking, *"What's the benefit of doing the right thing and obeying God? How does it help me here on earth?"* Well, the benefits come in many forms. God blesses us all differently. Each person's situation is different, so God blesses us according to our situation and how that affects His will and plan for our life and those around us. It may come in the form of favor and daily help. Our decision to obey may result in greater wisdom and discernment in our lives. It may come in physical blessings or spiritual peace by strengthening the Spirit inside you.

John 14:26 says, *"He [the Spirit] will teach you all things and bring to your remembrance all that I said to you."* Although Christ specifically referred to some of the things He told the disciples, the same promise He gave them, referenced in the book of John, still holds true today. The Holy Spirit has not gone anywhere. Some people want you to believe that God does not care about you or your life. That is false and could not be further from the truth. The Lord still cares and is still working today. The power and presence of the Holy Spirit are still at work today, according to our fellowship and walk with the Lord.

Understand as we go about our day, we need to remain under and within the baptism of the Holy Spirit. Don't leave your baptism in the past and leave the Spirit by the water.

GIVING U.P.
Thoughts

Conversation Eleven
PURPOSE

Can you find your purpose and build a stronger relationship with the Lord?

My intent in drafting this book is to stimulate a deep, burning desire within you to know God better than you do now—not merely to have a superficial awareness of Him but to truly experience and understand His presence in every aspect of your life. I want you to move beyond simply knowing of Him so that you can develop a vibrant, personal relationship with Him that transforms your heart and mind.

As you come to know the Lord more intimately, you will also begin to know yourself. This journey of spiritual discovery is not just about understanding divine truths but also about discovering what excites you, what nurtures your soul, and, most importantly, what God desires for you in every season of life. When you truly know the Lord, you begin to see the purpose behind your own existence, and that insight has the power to save lives—perhaps even your own. I didn't fully understand this purpose when I first began writing this book, but as I progressed, my eyes were gradually opened through constant interaction with the Lord. I discovered that deep, personal revelation can reframe how we view our challenges, our relationships, and our destiny.

This work is meant to be an invitation—a call to renew your commitment to a faithful walk with the Lord. I want you to embrace a mindset that refuses to give up on your spiritual growth, even when the journey seems long, or the challenges appear insurmountable.

There were moments in my own life when I felt overwhelmed, but by staying connected to God, I found renewed strength and clarity. I hope that as you read these words, you begin to see the value in seeking a stronger, more genuine relationship with your Lord and Creator, not only for your own benefit but also so that you can be a beacon of hope and support for others on their journey.

Throughout this process, I learned that knowing God changes everything. It opens your eyes to the beauty and purpose in every moment and allows you to recognize the gifts He has uniquely designed for you. When you invest in a deeper relationship with Him, you also learn to recognize the subtle ways He speaks to you—through scripture, through nature, and through the people around you. This relationship can guide you through even the darkest times, helping you to find joy, peace, and the courage to live a life that honors Him.

So, do not give up on your faithful walk with the Lord. Do not give up on your spiritual growth. Do not give up on yourself. Do not give up! Instead, seek an understanding and perspective that will ignite a passion within you—a passion to pursue a stronger relationship with your Lord and Creator. Let this renewed relationship not only transform your own life but also empower you to help others on their journey through life. The deeper you dig, the more you will discover that knowing Him truly makes all the difference.

ABOUT THE AUTHOR

Lionel P. Wesley is a native of Dallas, Texas, and a proud graduate of Duncanville High School, where he played baseball, basketball, and football. He went on to earn a Bachelor of Science in English from the U.S. Naval Academy and a Master of Arts in Defense and Strategic Studies from the U.S. Naval War College. During his military career, Lionel rose to the rank of Commander (CDR) in the United States Navy.

He is a devoted husband to Brittany Wesley and the proud father of two children—his son, Gabriel, and daughter, Ariana. When he's not engaged in work or family life, Lionel enjoys quality time with his loved ones, often found building Legos with his children or creating memories through everyday moments. He also treasures quiet time with God, regularly spending time in Scripture and in prayer.

It was through this deepening relationship with God

ABOUT THE AUTHOR

that the desire to write this book was born. Lionel's heart is to help others unlearn misconceptions and rediscover the truth of God's Word. His prayer is that through these pages, readers will be pointed back to Christ, grow in understanding of God's intent for believers, and walk boldly in the purpose God has placed within them.

CONNECT WITH THE AUTHOR

FACEBOOK   Lionel P. Wesley

www.ingramcontent.com/pod-product-compliance
Lightning Source LLC
Chambersburg PA
CBHW030453100526
44580CB00009B/115/J